Here's To
Your
SUCCESS

Here's To Your SUCCESS

JEFF KELLER

Attitude is Everything, Inc.
East Norwich, NY

ISBN 13: 978-0-9790410-2-0
ISBN 10: 0-9790410-2-3
LCCN: 2007903161

10 9 8 7 6 5 4 3 2 1

Printed in the United States of America

Published by Attitude is Everything, Inc.
P.O. Box 310
East Norwich NY 11732-0310

www.attitudeiseverything.com

Cover Design by Joni McPherson (www.mcphersongraphics.com)
Interior Design by Jill Ronsley (www.suneditwrite.com)

Acknowledgments

To God, for your loving guidance and for the many blessings you have bestowed upon me.

To my wife, Dolores, for her love and her support of my work every step of the way.

To Stuart Kamen, for his excellent editing of the vast majority of the essays in this book.

To the thousands of people who have communicated with me by mail, e-mail, and in person, to let me know how much you have benefited from these essays. I am so grateful for your support and encouragement.

Contents

A Personal Message from Jeff Keller

No matter where you are on your journey of self-development, I believe there is a reason why our paths have crossed here.

While I don't know you, there is one thing of which I am certain: this book contains principles that can dramatically improve your life. I can say that with confidence because these principles changed my life for the better — and they have done the same for millions of others.

In the mid-1980s I experienced a turning point in my own journey of self-development. I was dissatisfied with my career as an attorney and very discouraged. At that time, I knew little about attitude and success principles. I was "rescued" by these principles, and they opened up a wonderful new life for me.

Rest assured that I haven't figured out everything in life yet. We're all a "work in progress." But I know that the principles in this book can help you to become a happier person, a more successful person (no matter how you define success) and a person who makes a positive difference in this world.

This book is not about overnight success or getting rich without any effort. I've found that those things don't exist. Success requires discipline — developing new ways of thinking and acting. It is well worth your time and effort to develop this discipline.

For more than 10 years, I have distributed my essays online to people all over the world. In this book, I've chosen 62 of them to share with you. Enjoy the essays, apply their lessons and you'll create an extraordinary life.

Here's to YOUR success!

Jeff Keller

1

Here's Why "Attitude Is Everything!"

The greatest discovery of my generation is that human beings can alter their lives by altering their attitudes of mind.

— William James

Attitude is Everything. It's the name of my company, and it's a philosophy I endorse with every ounce of my being, because I know first-hand how this principle has changed my life for the better. And yet, in my travels, people come up to me and say, "Sure, attitude is important. But is it "everything"? Well ... I truly believe that it is.

For our purposes, let's take a very simple definition of a positive attitude. First and foremost, people with a positive attitude are **optimistic**. They focus on "can" instead of "can't." They see possibilities instead of limitations. Now, I'm the first to admit that success requires more than just a positive attitude—there are other principles you have to apply. But it all starts with attitude! Without a positive attitude, you can't tap into any of the other success principles. Your attitude is the foundation and the starting point for your success and fulfillment.

Let's examine how your attitude activates the other keys to success:

- **Confidence.** Can you be confident and persuasive if you're not optimistic? I don't believe so. The confident person believes in his or her abilities and strides forward with the expectation of success. Others can see and feel that confidence. Negativity breeds doubt and hesitancy.

- **Persistence.** We all know the value of making repeated attempts until we reach our objective. Why on earth would you persist if you didn't believe you'd succeed in the long run? Optimism leads to persistence. Negative people give up at the first sign of trouble because they feel there's no use in making further efforts.

- **Resiliency.** Getting back on your feet when you've been knocked down— that's surely one of the most important success principles. Those who are negative get even more pessimistic when things don't go as planned. Positive people get frustrated temporarily … and then they look for the opportunity or learning that comes from adversity. I've also discovered that those who are extremely positive don't resist life's events, curse their fate or bemoan how bad things always happen to them. Instead, they believe that everything happens for a reason. This approach helps them to overcome setbacks and "go with the flow."

- **Courage.** There's no sustained success without courage. When you believe you can do something, you have the courage to move forward despite being afraid. Negative people, on the other hand, tend to back away from their fears and thus sabotage their potential.

- **Enthusiasm and Energy.** Show me a person with a dynamic, positive attitude and I'll show you someone

4

who is energetic and, in all likelihood, enthused about what he or she is doing. These people have a spring in their step and you feel better just by being around them. How many negative people do you know that you'd describe as energetic and enthusiastic? How many negative people do you look forward to being around ... just because they give you such a boost each time you're with them? None, I'll bet. Negativity is an energy drain, while optimism is an energy enhancer.

◆ **Health.** This is one of those relationships that you have to experience for yourself to appreciate. We all know times in our lives when we got sick because we were under significant stress and consumed with negativity. Well, when I was in my 20s and had a negative attitude, I felt tired and battled a variety of minor ailments. The moment my attitude improved, my health improved. I looked and felt younger. The truth is, the cells of your body literally come alive when you're positive.

◆ **Encouraging Others.** As you begin to see and use more of your own potential, you're also able to see the greatness that lies within each individual. You have faith in the ability of others, and they pick up on that! Furthermore, the positive person is a far more effective leader. Would you want to follow someone who didn't believe in what they were doing ... or who expected a negative outcome? Of course not.

◆ **Gratitude.** When your outlook is negative, you tend to focus your attention on what is "wrong" with your life and you don't appreciate the beauty that is all around you. As you become more positive, you're in awe of the beauty and you walk around with a sense of wonder. Positive people appreciate everything more. They also find that they feel better when they're dwelling on their blessings, rather than complaining and finding fault.

- **Perspective.** This is a logical progression from your increasing feelings of gratitude. You appreciate the many positives in your life and recognize that they far outweigh any problems or temporary inconveniences. You don't make a big fuss over a flat tire or a lost sale because you know that they pale in importance to your health, your freedom and your friends and family.

- **"Approachability."** Think of the negative people you encounter every day. These individuals have a frown and you don't feel any warmth emanating from them. They create distance. The optimistic person, on the other hand, initiates a smile, and you tend to smile right back! You feel a certain connection with positive people and enjoy the time you spend with them.

- **Spiritual Growth.** People who make the commitment to develop their attitude invariably experience heightened spiritual awareness. Negative, unhappy people simply do not find a meaningful connection with a Higher Power. However, when you're filled with positive thoughts and feelings, you begin to appreciate yourself and others more. You begin to sense that there's a purpose behind everything and that you are part of a bigger plan. You also trust your intuition more and realize that you're receiving guidance on your journey.

I think you'd agree that this is a pretty impressive list of characteristics. And the way to access all of them is to build a more positive attitude. Never forget, however, that your attitude is a choice that you make every day. Decide to build an unshakable positive attitude. In the end, I think that you, too, will find that attitude IS everything!

2

The Secret to Being Lucky

Luck is preparation meeting opportunity.
— Elmer Letterman

Why do some people seem to have all the luck? They're always in the right place at the right time. Their businesses prosper. They get one fantastic promotion after another. *In short:* they enjoy phenomenal success. What explains it? Are they doing something special, or is good fortune selecting them by chance?

For a moment, let's put aside winning the lottery — which seems to be a random type of luck — and instead focus on those who consistently achieve extraordinary results in their lives. Often, we attribute their accomplishments to random luck. However, after studying the lives of these people, I've discovered that there's more to it than that. Indeed, these people seem to benefit from something I'll call "created luck."

People who create their own luck have certain traits in common. *Here, then, are the secrets for deliberately bringing luck into your life ...*

1. **Be proactive.** Show me a consistently lucky person and I'll show you someone who doesn't sit back waiting for good fortune to pay a visit. Indeed, lucky

people put themselves in a position to win by continually taking action in pursuit of their goals.

2. **Have a dynamic, positive attitude.** It has been proven that we attract what we think about most. People who get the breaks believe in themselves and in their abilities. They picture themselves reaching their goals and are secure in the knowledge that they'll master any and all challenges that come their way. To become a magnet for exceptional achievements, therefore, maintain a confident outlook and concentrate on success!

3. **Possess a burning desire.** Aside from being positive, lucky people are *passionate* about achieving their goals. They're always on the lookout to seize an opportunity, and you can bet they'll bring enthusiasm and energy to the quest.

4. **Be prepared.** Earl Nightingale said it superbly: if you are not prepared for your opportunity when it comes, the opportunity will only make you look silly. Lucky people are mentally, physically and emotionally ready to perform at their maximum. They are learners and hard workers. Whatever activity they're engaged in, you'll find them reading, practicing and picking the brains of successful people in that field. And they realize that the preparation must be done *before* the fantastic opportunity presents itself. Athletes may appear to be lucky at times, but don't forget the countless years of practice they put in.

5. **Display incredible persistence and a long-term perspective.** Most people want a lucky break and *they want it NOW!* If only success were that easy. Examine the lives of highly accomplished people and you'll find that virtually each one overcame years of

frustration and setbacks. In any profession, the few who refuse to quit when success is nowhere on the horizon are the ones who eventually achieve the "impossible."

6. **Pay your dues.** Lucky individuals are willing to start small and work their way up. For instance, in high school and in college, Michael Jordan wasn't the world's best basketball player. Likewise, Oprah Winfrey didn't begin her career as host of her own national television show. They developed their skills over time and *earned* the right to capitalize on their opportunities.

7. **Create crystal clear objectives.** Clarity is power. Lucky people know what they want to accomplish and can visualize the end result in vivid detail. They are motivated by an exciting picture that they seek to bring into reality. You just don't get very far with a vague notion that you want to be "happy" or "successful."

8. **Demonstrate flexibility.** Let's face it, no matter how well prepared you are, you can never anticipate *all* the setbacks and detours you'll encounter. Lucky people monitor their progress and make adjustments when appropriate. When a particular strategy isn't working, they don't complain or curse their bad luck; they just make a change. In addition, they are extremely open — and able to take advantage of — new opportunities which may arise as they pursue their original goal.

9. **Be a risk-taker.** This isn't about foolish, unprepared gambles. However, phenomenal, ground-breaking success is usually reserved for those who will venture into unknown territory.

In the end, successful people make their own luck. George Bernard Shaw may have said it best: "The people who get on in this world are the people who get up and look for the circumstances they want and, if they can't find them, make them."

3

The Boomerang

Work joyfully and peacefully, knowing that right
thoughts and right efforts will inevitably bring
about right results.

— James Allen

Whether you realize it or not, you are throwing the boomerang today. As you may know, a boomerang is an angular club which you toss away from you, and which eventually returns to you. In the game of life, you throw the boomerang daily, in the form of actions and behaviors which you send out into the world, and which return to you at some later date — often multiplied on the rebound.

You've probably heard this principle stated in different ways, including "What goes around comes around." Or the Biblical phrases "Give and it shall be given unto you" and "As you sow, so shall you reap."

But how does this principle apply to your day-to-day life? Simply put, if you treat others with love and respect, you will find that others will generally love and respect you. If you serve others, you will likely be served. Of course, this "law" also applies to negative behaviors. If you are critical and judgmental, don't be surprised when you are criticized and judged.

By the way, you don't always receive precisely what you send out. For example, you might steal money from others and rather than having money stolen from you in return, you could wind up in jail. But whatever the specific response, negative consequences always follow dishonest, unscrupulous actions, whereas positive results flow from fair and honorable efforts.

Before we continue, let's clear up some misconceptions about the boomerang principle. Many people don't believe in it because they fail to view it with a long-term perspective. The return for your actions is seldom immediate. In fact, there is often a long delay between your actions and the rebounding consequences.

So, if you feel that you are living a "good life" — that you are helping others, being loyal to your friends, creative in business, and loving to your family — and that you have yet to receive any great reward, don't despair. First of all, you might be overlooking the blessings that already exist in your life. Or, you may consider what Ralph Waldo Emerson believed about delayed rewards — that your good deeds are earning "compound interest" in the universal bank, building up value over time, and that, one day, you will receive handsome dividends. It is in this fashion that the universe rewards persistent people who diligently plod away at their ultimate goal ... and then (suddenly, it seems) attain outrageous success!

People also have trouble with the boomerang principle because they look for the return to come from the same person to whom they gave something. It doesn't usually work this way. You'll never know where the return will be coming from — or when it will arrive — but it always comes.

Perhaps the most useful way to observe this principle in action is to look at it "in reverse." In other words, focus on what is coming to you in life — and that will tell you what you have been sending out.

Thus, if you aren't receiving something that you want (e.g., friendship, love or honesty), consider the possibility that you have been withholding these things from those around you. What you withhold from others will be withheld from you. When you start giving these things, you will activate the flow back to yourself.

It's really quite simple. Send it out and receive it back. Think of the power which this puts in your hands to control what comes into your life!

How will you throw the boomerang today? The choice is yours.

4

Give Up the Grudge

*I never carry a grudge. You know why? While you're
carrying a grudge, they're out dancing.*

— Buddy Hackett

If you don't mind, I'd like to ask you a personal question. Here goes: Are you holding a grudge against someone? If you're like most of us, you can probably think of several people who you resent, or possibly even hate. Maybe someone lied to you, stole something from you, criticized you or inflicted physical or emotional pain upon you. It could have been a parent, relative, friend, co-worker, boss or even a total stranger.

For the purpose of this article, think about the person who you resent the most. As you contemplate this individual — and the way you were treated by him or her — how do you feel? I'll bet you are tense, uncomfortable, and your blood pressure is elevated. (This is your body's way of telling you that it doesn't like when you focus on hatred and resentment!)

Well, you ask, aren't grudges simply a part of life? After all, if someone hurts you, how are you supposed to react? There's no question that most of us have developed the habit of harboring ill feelings toward those who have hurt us. Yet, there *is* another choice we can make.

Take the example of former President Ronald Reagan who, in 1981, was shot and almost killed by John Hinckley. While in the hospital, Mr. Reagan told his daughter, Patti, that he knew his physical healing was dependent on his ability to forgive his would-be assassin. And he was able to do just that.

I've come to the conclusion that grudges are "internal poisons" that harm the individual who holds them far more than they affect the actual object of the hatred. Every minute that you hang on to resentment is damaging you physically, mentally, emotionally and spiritually. In addition, when you dwell on anger and resentment, you "block" your mind's creativity. Ideas flow best when you're calm and peaceful — not when you're consumed with hatred or revenge.

At this point, you might be saying, "But you don't know what so and so *did* to me!" That's right. I don't know. *So what!* The bottom line is your grudge is accomplishing *nothing* other than making you sick. Piling up "logical" reasons to maintain your ill feelings won't help one bit.

Let It Go

How, then, can we release our grudges? Denying your feelings surely won't work. If you feel hatred or resentment, admit it. It's really a question of how long you choose to hold on to your negative feelings. Each of us processes anger in a different way. Some are able to release a grudge after a short period of time. Others may take months or years.

*Here are some suggestions for letting go of **your** bitterness ... and for forgiving the person who hurt you. [NOTE: If you follow these steps, it doesn't mean that you now approve of the other person's behavior or that you've become best friends with him or her; you are merely releasing your ill feelings towards that individual.]*

1. **Make a list.** Write down the names of those for whom you feel anger or resentment. Don't confine the list to

major feuds—go back to silly arguments which you might have had during childhood. Take some time to do this. You'll probably be amazed at the size of your list! *(Now, pick the one person who generates the most negative emotions, and read on ....)*

2. **Identify the benefits of holding your grudge.** What is the grudge really accomplishing? Be honest. Write down all the ways your life is improved by holding this grudge. Most likely, your "benefits list" will be so short that you'll immediately see the futility of hanging on to the resentment.

3. **Forget about "right" and "wrong."** As you try to resolve these issues once and for all, focus only on releasing your ill feelings, not on trying to finally "win the argument."

4. **Don't set conditions.** You can't sit back and insist that the other person must apologize or call you first. It's up to you to make the first move. So, take the initiative and let go of your anger. *Remember, you're doing this to help yourself.*

5. **Go directly to the source.** Tell the other person that you are releasing the grudge. Explain that you are letting go of any resentment or ill feelings you possess toward him or her. You may choose to call, write or meet him or her in person. (If the other party is deceased, you can write a letter and then discard it.)

If you are truly coming from a place of warmth and compassion and if you have honestly let go of all anger and resentment, your communication with the other person will go much better than you might imagine. If, on the other hand, you are still trying to "win" your private battle, you are likely to create even more negative emotions.

In any case, the other person's reaction to your overture is not of primary importance. He or she may start screaming at you and slam down the phone. Or, you may find that this person wasn't even aware of your resentment to begin with. Whatever the response, however, you're going to feel much better after expressing your feelings and moving on!

Internal Release

Direct approaches involving the other person may not be necessary if you are able to **internally** let go of your anger. The following techniques may help you in this area.

6. **Consider the background of the other person.** The object of your resentment may not have received the love and attention that you've received throughout your life (maybe their parents were overly critical, etc.). This doesn't excuse their behavior, but it does make it easier for you to understand their actions. By thinking in this manner, you'll be more likely to feel compassion, as opposed to hatred. (For instance, according to Patti Davis, her father, Ronald Reagan never showed any hatred for John Hinckley. Rather, he expressed pity and referred to Hinckley as "misguided.")

7. **Contemplate (or pray for) the other person's well-being.** It may seem like a very odd thing to do, yet this very action can break the cycle of negative thoughts that you continually associate with the other person. So, try it now. Relax, inhale, and wish the other party health, happiness and prosperity. You may find this difficult at the outset. But stick with it and, if you really want to release the grudge, you'll eventually find that you are able to generate warm feelings for the other person.

8. **Visualize the tension leaving your body.** Close your eyes and get a picture of the resentment in your body. Make believe it's a tangible, definable object. What

color is it? Does it have a particular shape? Now, visualize that object or mass leaving your body and disintegrating into the atmosphere. Breathe deeply and feel the tension subside.

Don't Wait Any Longer

9. **Realize the ripple effect of your grudge.** In most cases—especially when family or in-laws are involved—your grudge has a significant impact on others. For example, let's say that you refuse to speak to your brother. You now make it awkward for family members to invite both of you to the same events. Be considerate and put your grudge aside. Everyone will benefit.

10. **Act NOW—before it's too late!** Broken relationships, especially with friends and family members, are a form of "unfinished business." Whether you realize it or not, a part of you wants to heal this relationship *during your lifetime.* Life is fragile, and you never know when someone will become ill, die or move thousands of miles away. If you don't mend the rift immediately, you may not get another chance. So, don't waste another minute—or you risk carrying around regrets for the rest of your life. *Here again, it doesn't matter if the other person welcomes your comments.* This is something you are doing to heal yourself.

11. **Speak to a counselor or therapist.** In certain instances, self-help methods alone are not enough to overcome negative emotions. You may have been the victim of abuse or suffered some form of serious physical or emotional trauma. If this is the case, seek assistance from qualified professionals who are skilled in counseling people in your particular situation.

Once you understand that grudges can only harm you, you won't find yourself holding onto them as often. So, what are you waiting for? Apply these techniques to the remaining people on your "grudge list." Keep in mind that when you let go of your negative feelings, you will feel a tremendous burden lifted from you. Now, do yourself a favor and give up the grudge ... *today!*

5

How to Attain
Your Heart's Desires

Nobody succeeds beyond his or her wildest expectations unless he or she begins with some wild expectations.

— Ralph Charell

Have you discovered your heart's desires? Better yet, have you made any progress toward achieving them?

Now, I know that the mere mention of the phrase "heart's desires" may conjure up an interesting image or two — like when a genie pops out of a magic lamp and grants you three wishes. While it may work this way in the movies, I've found that this isn't the case in the "real world." Rather, it is up to each of us to be attuned to what we truly want in our lives ... and to blaze our own trail to reach our fondest destinations.

While each person's path is unique, I'd like to share with you several principles that will help to guide you along this journey:

1. **Be open to discovery.** I don't think you find your heart's desires as much as they find you! We often get fooled into thinking we're identifying our heart's desires when, in fact, we're following what someone

else thinks is best for us ... or what our "logical mind" has figured out. This is NOT what I mean.

When you're positive and receptive, you'll find that you're "invited" to pursue a particular goal or to embark on a project. Then, it's up to you to accept the invitation and move forward, even if you're outside your comfort zone. For instance, I never set out to be a motivational speaker and writer. I just loved reading self-development books and listening to motivational audio programs — and then I began to get the idea of pursuing this career.

So, be open and don't try to judge how or when your heart's desires will come calling. You'll find that the paths that beckon you are those that make use of your unique talents and your unique personality — and often in a way that is of great service to others.

2. **Expand your beliefs.** Lots of people become frustrated when things don't work out the way they want. The problem is often a limited belief system. For example, many people complain about not making enough money or not attracting the right relationships. Yet, these same people keep saying (and believing) such things as "I never have enough money at the end of the month" or "All men are afraid of commitment." Your belief system (and your self-talk) must support what you wish to achieve. So, make sure your dominant thoughts are focused on what you want — as opposed to what you don't want.

3. **Go on a steady diet of positive emotions and feelings.** You accelerate your success and achieve your heart's desires when you not only think positive ... but also have positive feelings. I'm talking about strong positive feelings — the kind that make you tingle all over. This is the way you feel when you see a young child smile, or watch a beautiful sunset. Some of the

most powerful positive feelings are love, gratitude and forgiveness. When you access those feelings consistently, you become a magnet for wonderful things to come into your life.

4. **Let go of negative emotions.** Just as positive feelings help attract your heart's desires, negative emotions block you from achieving greatness. The typical emotions in this category are anger, hatred, resentment, jealousy and judgment. I wish I could tell you that I've conquered these negative emotions. But I haven't. What I *have* realized is that these emotions do not serve me in any way. Trust your body. How do you feel when you're angry or critical? You feel lousy and stressed out. You become a magnet for problems and illness. Note: I'm not suggesting that you deny your feelings. It's simply a matter of not dwelling on them for a prolonged period of time. Instead of getting bogged down in one of the negative emotions, *choose* one of the positive feelings discussed above and switch to a more productive frame of mind.

5. **Be flexible because your heart's desires will change.** You may think you know what you'll want a few years from now, but don't bet on it! A year from now, or even next week, you may get the urge to move in a completely new direction. Your interests will change. Your values will change. Your priorities will change. This is a *good* sign and shows you're growing and open to new avenues in your life. Each year, I seem to get a new project that excites me and draws my interest. I've learned not to question it. I just do it, and things always work out for the best.

6. **Follow the passion — not the money.** Don't get me wrong. Money is important, and I like material comforts as much as the next person. However, when

money is the primary force that drives you, you're unlikely to connect with your heart's desires and achieve fulfillment. Interestingly, you're also unlikely to accumulate much money. However, when you pursue a career or hobby that excites you, you're on the road to discovering your heart's desires and to living a satisfying life. In time, that's also the path most likely to bring you the material rewards you want.

7. **Get in "the flow."** You attract people and opportunities into your life as a result of your consciousness. At the beginning of our journey, we tend to think that we have to grit our teeth and fight to achieve our heart's desires. Yet, when we're in the flow of life, we manifest what we want much more easily — like guiding a canoe along with the current. Being in the flow is not the same as being passive and sitting back, however. You still put forth effort, but you find that when you're positive and pursuing your "correct" path, things fall in place. You meet people who can help you move forward. Sure, you encounter obstacles, but you know you'll overcome them. It's just a matter of time. If you're tense and struggling, you're probably "off course" and need to make some adjustments.

Please don't make the mistake of thinking that this article is about spiritual and emotional fulfillment only; the principles here will bring you material success as well. My main goal is to get you to think about how these principles are operating in your life — and whether you could make some changes to lead an even more successful, satisfying life.

One final point: the actual act of *achieving* your heart's desire is not always as exhilarating as you had anticipated. The real joy comes from the everyday actions you take — and what you learn and become along the way. It's a journey of growth and satisfaction you don't want to miss!

6

Is Conformity
Holding You Back?

We forfeit three-fourths of ourselves
to be like other people.

— Arthur Schopenhauer

In 1971, singer Rick Nelson was one of the performers at a rock revival concert held at Madison Square Garden in New York City. When it was his turn to perform, Rick Nelson sang some of his "old" hit songs — the music his fans had come to love and expect. He then sang some of his new material, which was quite different from his other music. Upon hearing the new songs, the audience booed and strongly showed their displeasure. Nelson was hurt and frustrated. Based on this experience in The Garden, he wrote the song "Garden Party," which became a big hit in 1972.

The song teaches an important lesson: namely, that we don't have to conform to the expectations of others. Rick Nelson's fans in 1971 wanted him to play only the "oldies." He wanted to branch out and try some new things. The song contains these well known lyrics: "Ya can't please everyone, so you got to please yourself."

This isn't a song that extols the virtues of being selfish or ignoring the wishes of those around us. Rather, it's about being true to yourself, even if some people won't like it.

The dictionary defines "conform" as "to act in accordance with prevailing standards or customs."

Let's examine the concept of conformity a little closer. There's no denying that most of our lives are spent conforming to standards set by others. That's not necessarily a bad thing. In fact, it's absolutely essential to the smooth operation of our society. Most of us conform to laws and ethical standards. We wear shoes, blouses or other clothing items every day, even though we didn't come up with these ideas. In school, our children are taught to raise their hands before shouting out a comment. All of these "customs" improve our lives, and we've decided to follow them.

However, not all acts of conformity serve us. Let's review some of the ways in which we conform, and see whether our lives are enhanced—or hampered—by doing so:

Belief Systems. From the time of our birth, we're influenced by the belief systems of those who surround us. And, in most cases, we've adopted those belief systems as our own. Were your parents risk takers? Are you a risk taker? Did any of your parents have a positive attitude? How would you describe your attitude? I'll bet that you're beginning to see a connection. Whatever beliefs may have been passed on to you, the crucial question is: do these beliefs enhance your life—or detract from your life?

Your views about money, marriage and a host of other issues are often the result of what you were told, as opposed to what you independently believe. But now that you know this, it's your choice whether to continue to live according to these beliefs, or to choose differently.

Career Choices. Some people receive direct pressure as to which career path to take—or they receive a subtle message along those lines. I had wonderful parents and they never told me what career to select. Yet, my parents grew up in the Depression and security was very high on their list of values. So, they encouraged me to go to graduate school and be a "professional." "Get the piece of paper [your degree] and they can never take that away from you." So, I "chose" to be a lawyer. It wasn't until a decade or so later and a lot of soul searching that I embarked on a different career path as a motivational speaker and author.

Looking back, it's clear that I conformed to my parents' wishes. In most instances, our parents steer us in a particular direction because they love us and think it would be best for us. But, as adults, we must ask if we're living based on someone else's wishes—or if we're following our own desires. If you have children, what messages have you given to them regarding their career options?

Behavior. Consider the way teenagers conduct themselves. Because of heavy peer pressure, youngsters are wary about how they act and whom they "hang out" with. For them, it's so important to be popular and accepted. As a result, it may be unacceptable to associate with those who are not part of the "in crowd." Adults play this game as well. We belong to groups and organizations that have certain traditions, hierarchies and rules that we may or may not agree with. Yet, we often keep our mouths shut and conform. After all, we don't want to "rock the boat."

How does it make you feel to conform to practices that at best make no sense ... or at worst are counterproductive? You don't have to "tell people off" or spill your guts on everything you disagree with. However, there are times when taking a stand will lead to positive change, and you'll feel a whole lot better about yourself for speaking up.

Clothing and appearance. This is one of the most prevalent areas where we conform. Here again, just about everything we wear is based on a standard set by someone else. Have you ever thought about the way we take our cues from others, such as fashion designers? They tell us that wide neckties are "in," so we go out and buy wide ties. The following year, they declare that narrow ties are "in," so we go out and buy them. People look at the hairstyles of famous celebrities and then run out to copy those styles. Does this really make a lot of sense to you?

Now, you might argue that in business and in our personal lives, we have to interact with people. And, if we don't follow some of these standards, then others will not view us in a favorable way. You're absolutely right. However, it's up to you to decide just how far this goes until you lose your individuality.

I'll offer these parting observations. To begin with, have a little more tolerance for those who think and act differently than you do. Celebrate their uniqueness, and learn from them. Secondly, give some thought to how conformity impacts your life. When you conform, you run the risk of surrendering your true self. You think and act as others dictate. You turn your back on your individuality, and deny the world the benefit of your unique talents and viewpoints.

So, take a careful look at the ways in which you conform. Hold onto those things that serve you. But, when every ounce of your being rebels against what you're thinking and doing, have the courage to break with conformity and to blaze your own trail. In doing so, you just might discover a lot about yourself and the life you were meant to live.

7

Energy Sells!

*If you're positive and enthusiastic,
people will want to spend time with you.*

— Jeff Keller

You're watching TV and channel surfing when you come upon what you recognize right away as an "infomercial." There's a guy on the screen telling you about this phenomenal new product. He can barely contain his enthusiasm. The camera then cuts away to people who have used this product. They are smiling and telling you all the benefits of this gadget.

Do you keep channel surfing? No, for some odd reason you keep listening to the infomercial. At one point, you feel like pulling out your credit card and ordering the gadget. Then, you come to your senses and say to yourself, "How often will I need a knife that can cut through my leather shoes?"

Why did you listen to the infomercial for several minutes? You were captivated by the energy of the people on the screen. They were incredibly dynamic and enthusiastic. And energy sells!

Energy sells not only when you're trying to persuade someone to buy your product or service. It also sells when it comes to interpersonal relationships. Let's say you're sitting at a table having dinner with a few people that you've never met before. You look to your left and see someone who, in your opinion, is physically attractive. You look to your right and see another person who is "average" looking.

Then, the dinner conversation begins. As it turns out, the "attractive" person has a very dull personality and shows very little energy. The "average" person speaks very enthusiastically about his or her career and travel experiences. You are captivated and enthralled. After the evening, aren't you going to see the "average" person as being much more attractive than you originally thought ... and the "attractive" person being much less so? Of course.

When you're energetic, you'll gain these benefits:

+ People will want to be around you.

+ People will be more receptive to your ideas.

+ People will be more likely to buy your product or service.

I think we can all tap into a vast supply of energy hidden within ourselves and here are some guidelines to help you do just that:

1. **Follow your passion.** The number one factor in harnessing your energy is to get involved doing things that you love to do. Ideally, you should work in a field that really excites you and makes you look forward to going to work each day. Now, I'm not telling you that you have to quit your job if you don't like your current position or line of work. But, it's crucial that you find some outlet, even if it's a hobby, where you can engage in activities that get your juices going. If you fill your days with boring activities or drudgery, you are cutting off your energy.

2. **Become more animated.** Movement is magical. If you watch young children, they are very animated and excited. Over the years, however, we learn to

suppress our natural exuberance. When that happens, our energy is reduced. So, loosen up and don't be rigid when expressing yourself with others. Let your enthusiasm shine through.

3. **Laugh!** Humor is a great energizer. So, when someone says something funny, don't be afraid to laugh. Likewise, don't hide your natural sense of humor. Nearly everyone responds well to laughter and it will make you feel better and more energized.

4. **Do it your own way.** Becoming more energetic doesn't mean you have to be loud! You can develop your own kind of energy. Now, the truth is, when you develop more energy and charisma, you **will** change in some ways. But, in most instances, you will not completely abandon your original personality.

5. **Maintain your physical health.** This one is fairly self-explanatory. If you have poor eating habits, get insufficient rest and don't exercise, it should come as no shock to you when you have little energy. You must take care of yourself physically to maximize your energy.

So, do you want people to respond more favorably to your ideas ... and to your sales presentations? If so, follow the energy boosters described above, and you'll find that more and more people will be sold on YOU!

8

How Reliable Are You?

As I grow older, I pay less attention to what men say.
I just watch what they do.

— Andrew Carnegie

D o you keep your word? Don't answer too fast — the truth may surprise you. When I say **keep your word**, what I really mean is: when you say you are going to do something, do you carry through and do it? *Within the time period that you promised?* Let's consider the following statements.

1. I'll mail the check to you **today**.

2. I'll e-mail the proposal and price quote **tomorrow**.

3. **Next week,** I'll call you and we'll meet for lunch.

Assume that it is Monday and you make each of the three statements above. You've kept your promise on statement #1 if, and only if, you mail the check on **Monday**. If you mail the check on Tuesday or Wednesday, then you have not honored your promise. If you haven't e-mailed the proposal and price quote by the close of business on Tuesday, you haven't kept your word. As for statement #3, most of us would confess to violating that one now and then. We say things like, "Let's have lunch together," or "You must come over sometime," when we know, full well, that we aren't going to follow up and make definitive plans to get together.

At this point, you might be saying to yourself, "What's the big deal?" "Does it really matter if I mail the check on Wednesday instead of on Monday — or if I e-mail the proposal on Thursday rather than on Tuesday?" I think that it makes a BIG difference and here's why.

Negative Consequences of Breaking Your Word

A. **Each inaccurate statement you make chips away at your credibility.** Don't underestimate the importance of reliability. People love to do business with those they can count on; those who do *exactly* what they say they'll do. When you make statements and fail to deliver on "small" things, people tend to believe that you won't deliver on more important items as well.

B. **"Close" is not enough if you want to achieve maximum results.** You might think that you are doing well because your conduct comes *pretty close* to matching your promises. If this is the case, the message you are sending out is, "When I tell you something, you can't rely on me to do *exactly* what I said, but I'll come pretty close." If you take that approach, don't expect to be as successful as you might otherwise be. It's true that some people will put up with your less-than-accurate statements. But, without question, others will be turned off and will not want to deal with you.

C. **What you regard as minor might be very crucial to someone else.** For instance, while it might not be a "life and death" matter to you whether the proposal and price quote is e-mailed on Wednesday instead of Tuesday, your prospective client may view it quite differently. For instance, this person might have solicited two proposals already and yours is the final one to be considered. You said that your proposal would be in hand by Tuesday; the client has planned to make a final decision on Tuesday evening. When your proposal doesn't arrive on time, the client makes a choice without considering yours.

Meanwhile, you wasted all day Wednesday formulating a spectacular proposal ... all for nothing. Remember, a prospective client won't always tell you about their plans. No matter how much research and preparation you do, you can't know everything that is going on in the other person's mind. Therefore, deviating from your promises, even slightly, can have serious consequences.

D. **When you fail to deliver as promised, you cause stress and aggravation to others.** Sometimes, we overlook the ripple effect of our promises. After all, people are making plans and promises based on the accuracy of our statements. If we let them down, they must let others down. For instance, let's say that one of my creditors is pressing me for payment. No problem, because *you said* you were sending out a check to me on Monday by overnight delivery. I figure that I'll deposit your payment on Tuesday and I tell the creditor to stop by my office on Thursday to pick up a check. When your check isn't delivered on Tuesday, I have to explain to my creditor that I'm going to let them down.

These situations are stressful and embarrassing. When you honor your promises, you make life easier for those counting on you — you are a stress re-ducer rather than a stress pro-ducer.

Action Steps for Improvement

The purpose of this article isn't to make you feel guilty and depressed about your failure to keep your word. The reality is that nobody keeps their promises 100% of the time. Thus, the focus is not on attaining *perfection*, but rather on **improvement**.

All of us can improve in this area and we should *begin by accepting where we are right now* — and, at the same time, make a commitment to become more reliable. What follows are some action steps to help you make significant strides in keeping your word on a more consistent basis.

1. **Treat every statement as a promise.** Few people treat their statements as iron-clad promises that **must** be kept. Yet, this orientation will contribute substantially to your success and to your ability to gain the cooperation of others. So, from now on, when a statement comes out of your mouth, it is a *promise* to be carried out. From this day forward, if you don't intend to do something, don't say you'll do it in the first place!

2. **Tone down your words until they are consistent with your actions.** Stop promising to do something in one or two days when you know that it will take a week. This is where most people get tripped up. They say what the other person wants to hear (e.g., "your order will be ready in two days") believing that this will create a favorable impression — which it does ... until they fail to honor their promise. And, the fact that you are "busy" is no reason to break your word. Take into account that you're busy **before** you make any commitment. Say only what you know you can live up to.

3. **If you can't meet your deadline, advise the other party *before* the deadline expires.** Common sense,

right? You would think so. Yet, this simple courtesy is frequently overlooked. After all, there will be times when, despite your best efforts — or because of emergency circumstances outside of your control — you won't be able to honor your promise. In these instances, contact the other party before the deadline has passed and explain the situation, re-committing to another deadline in the near future. Nine times out of ten, the other party will be very understanding and will appreciate that you took the initial deadline so seriously ... and that you were professional enough to call to reschedule.

By the way, keeping silent and hoping that they won't notice is a losing strategy. Believe me — they'll notice. Whether or not they say anything to you now, from this point on they'll think of you as unreliable.

By consistently keeping your word, you will stand out from the rest of the crowd. People will respect you and want to do business with you. And, you'll get plenty of referrals. Think about it: don't *you* like to do business with (and associate with) individuals who are trustworthy and honest?

Most importantly, when you bring your actions in harmony with your promises, you'll gain tremendous self-respect. You'll be acting with integrity, you'll feel better, and you'll perform at higher levels.

So, are you ready to make the commitment to improve in this area? Did you say "YES!"? Do I have your word on that?

9

The Devil
Didn't Make You Do It

*Take your life in your own hands and what
happens? A terrible thing: no one to blame.*

— Erica Jong

We're having a crisis in this country when it comes
to accepting personal responsibility. It seems that
nobody wants to be accountable for anything
anymore. Turn on any of the TV talk shows and all you see
are people blaming others for their plight. They're always
screaming that their lives are messed up because of their
boyfriends, ex-wives or parents. I've never heard any of the
guests say, "I created this mess in my life. It's all my doing."

Another pet peeve is the avalanche of lawsuits we see
today. If we fall in the supermarket, we sue the store. If we
slip on the sidewalk, we sue the property owner. I may have
a radical viewpoint here, but I've found that when someone
falls down, it is usually not the fault of the property owner,
but rather the person who fell down and wasn't being careful.
In our society, the new rule seems to be: if something goes
wrong in my life, I'll sue someone.

I Thought I'd Seen It All Until ...

Several years ago, I read about a lawsuit brought by a 56-year-old man in New York. The plaintiff, Mr. Barber, sued four fast food chains, claiming he became obese and suffered from other serious health problems from eating their fatty cuisine. He said "the fast food industry wrecked my life."

What could possibly justify such a lawsuit? Did employees from McDonalds break into Mr. Barber's home each day, hold him down and force Big Macs and fries down his throat? No, it didn't happen that way. Mr. Barber made the **choice** to eat fast food regularly and then sought to blame the fast food chains for his heart attacks, high blood pressure and elevated cholesterol.

Mr. Barber's lawyer said that the fast food companies are deceiving people by not telling them that this food is detrimental to their health. Come now, can you reach the age of 56 years in this society and really believe that Whoppers and chocolate shakes have the same nutritional value as broccoli? Any 10 year-old knows that chicken nuggets, fries and hot apple pies are not health food.

Maybe I should have seen this coming. After all, people chose to smoke, damaged their health, and successfully sued the tobacco companies. Who do *you* think bears the responsibility? The tobacco companies that sold the cigarettes or the smokers who chose to smoke, knowing of the health risks? What's next? Sue ice cream manufacturers if I eat too many hot fudge sundaes? Sue beer manufacturers if I drink too much beer? Sue the municipalities who maintain the beaches if I cut my foot on a shell while walking on the sand?

Now, don't get me wrong. I'm all for corporations taking responsibility and warning people of potential dangers. When someone conceals damaging health information or misrepresents the truth, they should be punished accordingly. We want property owners, for instance, to keep the premises safe and free of hazards. But we've taken this thing way too far, assigning blame whenever we're careless or make poor choices.

This shirking of responsibility exerts more influence than you might think. Without even knowing it, we're being conditioned to assign blame rather than to make wiser choices. And this outlook keeps us stuck and prevents us from getting the results we desire.

Before you jump on the bandwagon to criticize Mr. Barber and those like him, let's recognize that *all* of us fall prey to assigning blame for our ineffective strategies. I'm no exception. I'll bet there's something in your life that's not going as you want. And instead of taking responsibility and making adjustments, you're blaming someone else—perhaps your spouse or your boss—for your lack of success.

Maybe your business hasn't grown as you planned, and you're convinced that the problem is the sluggish economy. Perhaps you're not exercising enough and you attribute it to the fact that you're just too busy. Even the most highly successful people have what I call "pockets of irresponsibility." In other words, they take a proactive stance in most areas of their life, but in a few areas, they blame someone or something outside of themselves for their lack of progress.

Are there any areas of your life where you feel stuck or where you haven't gotten the results you wanted? If so, the chart on the following page may be helpful. In the left column, list several objectives that you've been struggling with lately. In the middle column, identify the obstacles that are standing in the way of reaching that goal. In the right column, list the steps you can take immediately to move in the desired direction.

What I Want to Accomplish	What Prevents Me / Obstacles	What I Can Do

If you feel that there's absolutely nothing you can do, then either give up that objective, or at the very least, stop whining about it. You're wasting energy needlessly.

When you see a co-worker or friend assigning blame for something, steer them back to possible solutions to their dilemmas. Encourage that person to take responsibility. When you're frustrated with something in your life, don't think blame. Don't think excuses. Blaming others and making excuses will not improve your life, and I doubt you'll find your magical solution in a lawsuit, either. Each of us has been blessed with a powerful, creative mind that can do so much more than we give it credit for. As Winston Churchill said, "The price of greatness is responsibility." Take responsibility and move forward on the road to greatness.

10

How to Develop a Healthy Perspective

Don't sweat the small stuff.

— Richard Carlson

Everyone experiences problems from time to time. But the way in which people respond to their troubles can vary greatly. Take the example of two drivers, each of whom gets a flat tire on the way to work. The first motorist's whole day is ruined. He mumbles about his rotten luck for hours, spreading blame wherever he can and accomplishing very little at work. The other driver, however, treats the flat tire as a minor inconvenience. He has it repaired and quickly moves on, proceeding to have an enjoyable, productive day.

Each encountered the exact same problem. So, why did one driver get so upset while the other handled the situation with ease? What distinguishes them is their *perspective.*

The dictionary defines perspective as "the capacity to view things in their true relation or relative importance." Think about the people you know. Do you have any friends or co-workers who continually dwell on petty nonsense, such as who has the larger office window? And how about those who sever ties with close family members because of a dispute over the seating arrangements at a wedding? It's clear that these individuals have lost sight of the "relative importance" of things!

Too many people blow their problems way out of proportion, devoting precious mental energy to situations which do not carry "life or death" consequences. Virtually all of us will fall into this trap on occasion, but those who spend the least amount of time obsessing on trivial circumstances are likely to accomplish far more — and be happier in the process.

Yet, perspective encompasses more than just steering clear of petty upsets. It suggests that you've considered your place in the world and that you appreciate "the big picture." As you widen the lens of your perception, you'll experience less tension, improve your attitude, develop keener insight into the meaning of your life, and most likely enjoy greater material success as well. The question, then, becomes: *how* can we develop more perspective?

Well, one surefire way is through encountering and overcoming adversity. Dealing with difficult situations leaves you with a new outlook about what is truly important in your life. If, for example, you're faced with a life threatening illness, poor service in a restaurant will no longer seem very crucial.

Fortunately, you don't have to wait for a major catastrophe in order to gain perspective. Here are some suggestions to broaden your outlook which you can implement right away:

1. **Look at your problem in the context of your entire life.** Ask yourself: How important is this difficulty in the overall scheme of things? What will this matter ten years from now? Okay, so you have a leak in your bathroom. It won't significantly affect the rest of your life. Or, let's say a prospective sale falls through. Sure, you're disappointed, but it isn't the end of the world. The key is to see the problem for what it is — and not let it dominate your thinking for an entire day, week or month.

2. **Think often about how you fit into the "big picture."**
   Ask yourself, *Why am I here? What is my mission in life? Am I following my purpose? Am I resisting a path that continues to beckon me?* These are not silly, philosophical questions which only applied to Plato and Socrates. I'll be the first to admit that I never used to think about such issues. But I do now ... and it has enriched my life tremendously. When you begin to contemplate these questions, you'll pay less attention to petty annoyances — and be able to spend more time on things that will help you be a better person and make a more significant contribution.

3. **Wake up to the miracles all around you.** Whether you realize it or not, you are part of an extraordinary universe. Spectacular, mind-boggling things are happening every second. For instance, you breathe, your heart beats and you digest food all without any conscious effort. Tulips know when to pop up through the ground at precisely the right time each and every year. The earth rotates ... the sun rises and sets ... the seasons change. All part of a wondrous, never ending cycle. So, shake your ho-hum attitude and begin to appreciate the amazing intelligence guiding the universe!

4. **Be open to the idea that everything happens for a reason.** If you doubt this principle, speak to people who, in your view, are positive and successful and who also seem to have peace of mind. Ask them if they believe that everything happens for a reason. Then, ask those who answer with an enthusiastic "YES" to explain why they feel that way.

5. **Extend yourself to others.** We tend to get mired in our own problems, turning inward and growing depressed and frustrated. Finding ways to serve and

help others will make you feel better and broaden your understanding about the interconnectedness of all human beings. Even something as simple as offering a few encouraging words to someone else can make a world of difference — to them and to you.

6. **Interact on a regular basis with those facing serious challenges**. For example, volunteer each week in a local hospital and spend time with those who are ill. Or, donate your time serving meals in a soup kitchen. In either case, you'll be helping others while at the same time learning just how well off you are!

7. **Redirect your focus to the many blessings in your life.** Are you in reasonably good health? Do you have your eyesight and mobility? Is there a roof over your head and enough food in the refrigerator? There are many people who do not enjoy these gifts and who would gladly trade places with you. So, focus on the many things for which you are grateful. To reinforce this idea, take the back of an index card and write "Count Your Blessings" or "I have so much to be grateful for." Place the card where you'll frequently see it, such as on your desk, in your car or on the bathroom mirror.

8. **Be around people who have a healthy outlook**. We are influenced by the company we keep. Therefore, try to spend more time with people — be they friends, relatives or co-workers — who seem to put things in perspective. These individuals rarely complain, can easily distinguish between what's important and what's not, and are a joy to be around.

9. **View every problem as an opportunity for growth.** Too often, we see our difficulties as negative experiences which are there to punish us and cause pain. As

you look back on your life, you'll find that many problems and painful situations led to personal growth and improved conditions. Maybe you lost a job which in turn led you to a better position. Or a relationship ended but you wound up in a more fulfilling one. So, develop a strong belief that the "bad" experience is there to help you in some way. Don't curse your challenge; instead, look for the lessons or opportunities which your problems are showing you.

10. **Watch your mouth!** Do you frequently whine and complain ... or broadcast your ailments and minor irritations to everyone who crosses your path? Griping reinforces your problems, makes you feel more miserable and alienates others. Find something positive in your life — or in the other person's life — to talk about instead.

11. **Cultivate your spiritual connection.** I have found that the vast majority of people with healthy perspectives possess strong spiritual beliefs. Without belief in a Higher Power, much of life appears cruel and without purpose. As you tune into your spiritual nature, you gain a sense of purpose, receive more intuitive guidance, and are able to see the reasons behind the patterns in your life. Each of us, at the core, yearns to develop a connection with our Higher Power. It gives us security, confidence and peace of mind.

12. **Every day, read literature that expands your perspective.** It might be a spiritual book, like The Bible, or stories of people who have overcome tremendous obstacles. Keep reading whatever builds faith, love and strength for you. The key is daily repetition.

13. **Put yourself in physical surroundings where you can "get away" from everyday stress.** Changing your environment can give you a fresh, relaxed point

of view. Maybe you like to sit on the beach or take a walk in the woods. Find scenery that allows you to release tension and think creatively ... and go there as much as possible.

14. **Exercise.** Aside from the physical benefits to our bodies, exercise provides release from stress and clears our thinking. I'm amazed at those who say, "I don't have time to work out." That's like saying, "I don't have time to be healthy!" Exercise does wonders to get your mind off your problems and makes you that much more able to handle stress as it occurs thereafter. So put exercise on your schedule *today!*

15. **Lighten up and laugh.** We take ourselves and our activities far too seriously. Find the humor in every-day situations and, most importantly, be willing to laugh at yourself. The very act of smiling and laughing makes us feel better physically and reduces tension.

16. **Simplify your life and restore balance.** Easy to say, but not so easy to implement. Sometimes, we get overextended, taking on too many responsibilities or projects. We ignore loved ones and even our own health. So, maybe it's time to say "NO" to the next project or demand on your time. Which is really more important — another volunteer committee as-signment or spending time with your children?

As you gain perspective, you'll find that your list of what is truly important will continue to narrow. As we mature, we tend to develop a broader outlook; yet there will be times when we become preoccupied with our difficulties and fail to see the larger issues. Therefore, we must constantly work at it.

Yes, maintaining perspective requires discipline. But the benefits — less tension, better relationships, greater peace of mind and more — are well worth the effort!

11

What Does "Created Equal" Mean?

To me, there is no difference whether
president, beggar, or king.

— The Dalai Lama

Written in 1776, the Declaration of Independence remains one of the most important documents ever created. As you probably know, it includes the following language:

"We hold these truths to be self-evident, that all men are created equal, that they are endowed by their Creator with certain unalienable Rights, that among these are Life, Liberty and the pursuit of Happiness."

Don't worry—no history quiz here! Instead, I'd like to invite you to explore the concept that "all men are created equal." At first glance, it seems to be one of those profound truths that is almost impossible to deny. But how many of us treat others according to this principle? Do we conduct our business or our lives applying the "all men are created equal" principle? All too often, our actions show that we don't, in fact, believe in this principle. I confess that I too have fallen short here as well.

The Spiritual Perspective

Imagine that your days on Earth have come to an end. Suddenly, you're face to face with God, who says the following: "Throughout your life, you treated the people with money and titles much better than the ones with little money or status. Congratulations! You seem to understand that I don't value each person the same, and that I favor those who have acquired assets or have large offices."

Do you believe there's any chance you'd hear that? No, because you know at the core of your being that all people ARE created equal, and that the Creator who gave you life also created every other person who crosses your path.

So how does this principle translate into the real world? Here are just a few examples:

Networking and Social Events. At a networking meeting, a woman who you're talking to suddenly sees someone else in the room she (apparently) feels is "more important" than you, and abruptly ends your discussion to approach the other person. How do her actions make you feel? You might argue that "business is business" and that people attend networking events to get new clients, not make chit-chat. Still, her "all people AREN'T equal" attitude comes across as rude.

Now, I'm not saying that you should spend equal time with everyone at these events. I do suggest that you treat everyone you meet with the same level of sincerity, professionalism, and common courtesy. Not only will you feel better about yourself, how you treat others almost always dictates how others treat you. What you sow, so shall you reap. Treat others as not worthy of your full respect, and you will be treated with little respect, too.

Interaction with Co-workers. Can you honestly say that you treat every person in your organization with the same level of respect? Does a call from the CEO carry the same weight as a call from someone you perceive as "lower" on the organizational chart? Do you give some people your undivided attention while "tuning out" others? It's always easy to justify treating people unequally...until you're on the receiving end.

Why don't we treat people equally? Here are two primary reasons:

1. **EGO.** Your ego sees others as being "separate" from you. You feel that you have to compare yourself with others and always come out "on top." The ego leads you to believe that by establishing "superiority" over others, you will be happy. Of course, this doesn't bring you lasting satisfaction no matter how much you accumulate. There is always someone who acquires more than you, who is more attractive than you, or who has a more prestigious title.

2. **MONEY.** We feel that we'll advance more quickly and earn more money if we treat the "higher ups" better simply because they possess the power to reward us. We believe that those on our level or below (on the organizational chart) have little influence in shaping our destiny. Now while it's possible that you might make more money by treating people "unequally," is this the legacy you want to leave? Can you really compartmentalize your life into "work" and "other" and justify not treating people equally when you wear your "work" hat?

My father, now deceased, taught me some important life lessons. He didn't teach by giving lectures. He simply led by example. Social or economic status meant little to my dad. He enjoyed talking with janitors as much as CEOs. Regardless of the person's status, my father took a genuine interest in the person, wanting to know about his or her family and background. He respected everyone and looked down on no one. My dad earned a good living. Could he have made more money by devoting more attention to the "important" people? Perhaps. But he didn't select that path, preferring instead to earn a little less and do right by others.

This week as an experiment, take a different perspective with those who cross your path. See everyone you meet as part of the same human family, from the beggar in the street to the person mopping the floor to your company's CEO. The same Higher Power created each of these individuals. Put into practice the truth expressed in the Declaration of Independence, namely that "all men are created equal." When you do what is right, you can't go wrong.

12

How to Handle Criticism

To avoid criticism, do nothing, say nothing, be nothing.

— Elbert Hubbard

There's no denying it: criticism can (and often does) hurt. But no matter what you do in life, you expose yourself to the possibility of being judged unfavorably. Even if you try to remain in the background, avoiding all confrontation, you still must make decisions — minor ones, maybe, like when to eat and what you wear. And, rest assured, not everyone will agree with your choices.

So, since you are going to receive criticism no matter what, let's take a closer look at how you can best handle (and even *benefit from*) it!

The next time you are criticized, consider the following points:

1. **Criticism is often nothing more than a reflection of personal preference.** Again, regardless of what you do, *somebody* won't like it. For instance, to get feedback from the audience at my seminars, I often hand out speaker evaluations. Without fail, two or three people will say that they wish there had been *more* time for audience participation during my

presentation; at the very same program, two or three others will say that they wish there had been *less* time spent on group involvement. Accept that people have diverse backgrounds, preferences and interests. You won't please everyone, so don't even try.

2. **Don't take it personally.** Sure, this is easier said than done. However, the critic generally isn't trying to prove that you have no value as a *person*. Rather, they're revealing their dislike of your idea or your performance. Let them have their opinions. In the end, *you decide* whether or not to let another person's remarks bother you.

3. **Strive to *learn* from their words.** Find some truth in their statements — even if only a shred. Usually, there is some accuracy in critical comments. The critic may not be tactful, and the remarks may be greatly exaggerated, but there is often helpful information which you can glean. It's your job to seek out this kernel of truth and benefit from it! For example, let's say your spouse accuses you of "never" being on time. While this statement is not entirely accurate, you should still consider in what ways, if any, you might improve your punctuality.

4. **Don't critique the critic.** It's an equally bad idea to adopt a "consider the source" attitude. Even if someone is generally untrustworthy or, for whatever reason, you don't get along with him or her, it doesn't mean that their comments will always be completely without merit.

5. **Don't be defensive.** Resist the temptation to argue with the critic. While it's only natural to try to prove that you are "right" and that the other person is "wrong," this generally gets you nowhere. (Of course,

there will be some instances where it's important to establish that you won't tolerate *abusive* remarks and that you deserve to be treated with respect. Use your best judgment.)

6. **Accept that many people focus only on negatives.** The critic rarely gives a full, accurate assessment. He or she tends to report only the negatives, even if there are plenty of positives to mention as well. Recognize that some people simply think it's unnecessary to tell you what you've done *right*. Instead, they focus only on "helping" you — which, to them, means "correcting" you.

7. **Realize that vicious, harsh comments come from people who are unhappy with themselves.** Here again, there might be a shred of truth or something you can learn from the criticism. But I've found that mean, angry, insulting remarks spring from unhappy, insecure people. They have to vent their anger and frustration on someone and *you've* been chosen as today's target! Don't let these people bring you down. **NOTE:** If you *repeatedly* receive harsh words from others, it's not a coincidence. You are attracting criticism based on your beliefs and your level of self-esteem. Take responsibility and look inward at what you can change to achieve more harmonious relationships with those around you.

Remember: not everyone will like you, your goals or your actions. But don't let the fear of criticism stop you from doing what you want. Accept criticism as part of life, and learn from it where possible. And, most importantly, stay true to *your own values and convictions. If others don't approve, so what!*

13

There's a Lot Riding on Your Self-Esteem

Until I started treating myself right,
I never ran into people who treated me that way.

— Unknown

There's a lot of talk about self-esteem ... and for good reason. Your self-esteem has a significant affect on every area of your life. Your self-esteem will affect the level of career success you attain. Your self-esteem will affect the mate you attract and the quality of all your personal and business relationships.

But what, exactly, *is* self-esteem? It's your own *feeling of worth* as a human being — the degree to which you like and value yourself and feel comfortable inside your skin. Author and speaker Jack Canfield has said that "self-esteem is based on feeling capable and feeling lovable."

In assessing your self-esteem, your answer to this question will provide much insight: "What do I *deserve* in life?" If you have low self-esteem and feel unlovable, undeserving or inadequate, you will tend to attract people and events that confirm your poor opinion of yourself. It's as if you emit a signal which says, "I don't like myself and I don't deserve much." Others pick up on this signal and treat you accordingly.

Fortunately, the reverse is also true. If you have high self-esteem and regard yourself as lovable, capable and deserving of life's best, you tend to bring into your life the people and circumstances that confirm your positive feelings of self-worth.

A Closer Look

Before going any further, let's differentiate high self-esteem from egotistical conceit or narcissistic love. Contrary to popular notion, conceited people or those who brag about themselves and view others as inferior actually have very *low* self-esteem. These people don't feel good about themselves ... and so they boast, put others down, and/or resort to intimidation in an attempt to convince others — and themselves — that they are valuable people.

Genuine self-esteem is a healthy, positive love and acceptance of yourself. When you truly love and appreciate who *you* are, you extend that love and warmth to others. You want to build up other people, not tear them down. When you have high self-esteem, you no longer view life as a fierce competition where you "win" by diminishing others; instead, you recognize that you "win" by contributing positively to the lives of those around you.

At this point, you may be wondering about the origin of your self-esteem. Unquestionably, your self-esteem is largely influenced by your childhood experiences. Young children are very impressionable and are likely to accept what they are told repeatedly. While some of the messages they receive may be beneficial, others may be limiting or destructive. Therefore, when children are given messages (by their parents, for instance) which suggest that they are not capable — perhaps they are frequently criticized or warned not to try new things — they might conclude that they are inadequate or have certain limitations. Ultimately, as adults, they are held back by the false beliefs that they accepted about themselves early on in life.

The consequences of this are extremely damaging. For example, at times we may feel that we *can't* accomplish certain tasks ... that we are inferior or just *not good enough* to apply for certain jobs ... or that we *don't deserve* to have a happy marriage or to get that promotion. These feelings are self-fulfilling prophecies. Only when we can release our self-limiting beliefs and negative feelings and replace them with positive feelings of self-love and acceptance, can we open up a new set of possibilities for our lives.

You Are Responsible

Once you're an adult, *you* are the only person responsible for your self-esteem — it does you no good to *blame* your parents or anyone else. Unlike a child, you can now choose which messages you accept and which you reject. As Eleanor Roosevelt said, "No one can make you feel inferior without your permission." Others can assist in raising your self-esteem, but the bulk of the effort must be yours.

Building high self-esteem is a **process**, not something you can develop overnight. Yet, I sincerely believe that every person has the capacity for high self-esteem. The question is, are you ready to make a commitment to increase your self-esteem? [Note: For some people, counseling or therapy with a qualified professional may be appropriate, especially if you have suffered some type of abuse or trauma.] *What follows are 11 valuable steps to help you boost your self-esteem.*

STEP #1: Stop comparing yourself with other people.

There will always be some people who have more than you, and some who have less. If you play the comparison game, you'll run into many "opponents" you can't defeat. Then you'll feel lousy and inadequate. Instead, compete only with yourself and strive to be the best you can be. You are unique and have your own path to follow.

STEP #2: Stop putting yourself down.

You can't develop high self-esteem if you continue to repeat negative phrases about yourself and your abilities. Whether speaking about your appearance, your career, your relationships, your financial situation, or any other aspects of your life, avoid self-deprecating comments. These put-downs only reinforce your own negative feelings and lower your self-esteem.

STEP #3: Accept all compliments with "thank you."

Have you ever received a compliment and replied, "Oh, it was nothing"? When you reject a compliment, the message you give to yourself is that you are not worthy of the praise. In the future, respond to *all* compliments with a simple "thank you."

STEP #4: Use affirmations to enhance your self-esteem.

On the back of a business card or small index card, write out a statement such as "I like and accept myself" or "I am a valuable, lovable person and deserve the best in life." Carry the card with you. Repeat the statement several times during the day, especially at night before going to bed and after getting up in the morning. Whenever you say the affirmation, allow yourself to experience the positive feelings you would have if your statement were true. For further reinforcement, hand-write the statement on a piece of paper at various times during the day.

STEP #5: Associate with positive, supportive people.

When you are surrounded by negative people who constantly put you and your ideas down, your self-esteem is lowered. On the other hand, when you are accepted and encouraged, you feel better about yourself. Therefore, put yourself in the best possible environment to raise your self-esteem.

STEP #6: Make a list of your past successes.

This doesn't necessarily have to consist of monumental accomplishments. It can include your "minor victories," like learning to skate, graduating from high school, receiving an award or promotion, reaching a business goal, etc. Read this list often. While reviewing it, close your eyes and recreate the feelings of satisfaction and joy you experienced when you first attained each success.

STEP #7: Make a list of your positive qualities.

Are you honest? unselfish? helpful? creative? Be generous with yourself and write down at least 20 positive qualities. Again, it's important to review this list often. Most people dwell on their inadequacies and then wonder why their life isn't working out. Start focusing on your positive traits instead, and you'll stand a much better chance of achieving what you wish to achieve.

STEP #8: Start giving more.

I'm not talking about money. Rather, I mean that you must begin to give more of yourself to those around you. When you do things for others, you are making a positive contribution and you begin to feel more valuable, which, in turn, lifts your spirits and raises your own self-esteem. Some suggestions: do some volunteer work or lend assistance to a worthy cause; spend some time with a friend or neighbor who is ill or going through a difficult period; offer to help a family member (who you wouldn't usually offer to help) on a personal project.

STEP #9: Get involved in work and activities that you love.

It's hard to feel good about yourself if your days are spent in work that you despise. Self-esteem flourishes when you are engaged in work and activities that bring you joy and make you feel valuable. Even if you can't explore alternative career options at the present time, you can still devote your leisure time to hobbies and activities that you find stimulating and enjoyable. One thing is certain: sitting home and moping — or complaining about your miserable day at work — will not raise your self-esteem.

STEP #10: Be true to yourself.

Live your own life — not the life others have decided is best for you. You'll never gain your own respect and feel good about yourself if you aren't leading the life *you* want to lead. If you are making decisions based on getting approval from friends and relatives, you are not being true to yourself and your self-esteem is lowered. When you pursue your heartfelt desires and dreams, your self-esteem and self-respect increase dramatically.

STEP #11: Take action!

You won't develop high self-esteem if you sit on the sidelines and back away from every challenge in your life. When you take action — regardless of the ensuing result — you feel better about yourself. When you fail to move forward because of fear and anxiety, you will be frustrated and unhappy — and you will undoubtedly deal a damaging blow to your self-esteem.

The "real you" is a magnificent, unique being with enormous potential and a tremendous capacity for experiencing love of yourself and extending that love to others. As your self-esteem grows, this "real you" will emerge. You will begin to take more risks and not be afraid of failure; you won't be as concerned with getting the approval of others; your relationships will be much more rewarding; you'll pursue activities that bring you joy and satisfaction; and you will make a very positive contribution to the world.

Most importantly, high self-esteem will bring you peace of mind ... because when you are alone, you'll truly appreciate the person you're with — yourself.

14

Pay Attention to the Details

Beware of the man who won't be bothered with details.
— William Feather

On my way home from the gym on Sunday morning, I used to stop at a well-known drug store chain to buy the Sunday newspaper. While there, I almost always picked up other merchandise, sometimes spending up to $40. On a recent occasion, however, when I returned home, I found that a section of the newspaper was missing. I discovered the same thing the following week.

The next Sunday, I brought the problem to the store manager's attention. He replied that "the kid who puts the sections together is in a hurry," as if this was a minor, unimportant error.

Yet, it wasn't minor at all. You see, I no longer stop at that store to buy the Sunday paper, which also means that I don't purchase other items there as well. After all, there are plenty of other places that sell toothpaste. This store lost my business because they weren't paying attention to the details.

Let me share a second example. Many years ago, I had a speaking engagement that was scheduled to start at 7:30 p.m. The only equipment I requested was a microphone and a slide projector. I had asked someone at the conference center how early I could get into the room before my presentation to make sure that everything was set up properly and functioning. I was told that the room would be opened around 7:00 p.m. Knowing what can go wrong in these situations, I politely requested that the room be opened earlier and that a technician be on hand to handle any last minute glitches. My request was granted and I was able to get into the room at 6:00 p.m.

Here's what happened. The slide projector in the room was not working. About 20 minutes later, they brought in another machine. Once again, it didn't work. About 15 minutes later, they located another projector. The first slide came right up on the screen. Then, I tried to advance to the next slide. Nothing happened. As it turned out, the remote control was not working. About 10 minutes later, another remote control device was found. Finally, everything was working properly ... and I still had about 30 minutes before the program was to begin. In the end, the presentation went very well and the equipment performed perfectly.

But, what would have happened if I couldn't enter the room before 7:00 p.m.? I'd have had to choose between two unpleasant options: delaying the program to try to get the equipment replaced, or abandoning the equipment entirely and doing my program without it. In either case, I would have done a disservice to my audience — all because I hadn't paid attention to the details.

Sometimes, we get so caught up in our product or service that we forget all of the other so-called "little things" that are part of the process. For instance, would it matter if you served the greatest food in your restaurant if the restrooms were filthy and without hand towels? Business would suffer immediately. Or, even if the food was delicious and the place was immaculate, would people continue to patronize your establishment if the waiter or cashier was consistently nasty to them? I doubt it.

So, what does all of this have to do with *you?* I'll bet that there are a lot of things you do at work that might seem "minor," but which, in fact, have far-reaching consequences. That's why it's so important to examine every aspect of your work on a regular basis and to make sure that each task favorably impacts your company's clients or customers.

Take a moment now to look at each component of your work. Do you arrive on the job dressed in a way that reflects well on yourself and your company? Do you let your clients know when you are running behind schedule for a meeting? Are there any changes you could make to your invoices to make them easier for customers to understand and process? Is there something you could do to make a coworker's job easier?

These may seem like insignificant items, but they have a profound affect on your company's bottom line ... and on your career.

If I'm a customer, I want to do business with people who pay attention to the details. If I'm an employer, I want to hire (and promote) people who realize that every task and communication either adds to — or subtracts from — the company's success. Ultimately, when we serve others (which is the essence of any business) there is no such thing as a minor detail. By paying attention to the "little things," we build a solid foundation for consistent success.

15

Be Aware of Your Patterns

There are no accidental patterns.

— Jeff Keller

I f you're like most people, you've probably noticed some *patterns* in your life. By "patterns," I mean situations that seem to show up over and over again; the cast of characters may change a bit, but the end results remain the same.

In and of themselves, such patterns aren't necessarily good or bad. They can be the source of boundless joy or tremendous frustration, economic abundance or financial struggle. In fact, it's quite likely that you have both *positive and negative* patterns in your life right now.

For instance, maybe you've worked for numerous bosses who have been very critical of you. No matter what company you're with, the same result occurs. This is a pattern.

If you honestly analyze your life, you will see that **you have created** (and continue to create!) *many* patterns — some that serve you and others that hinder your progress.

At the root of most patterns is a belief system (your expectations about what you can achieve) and your level of self-esteem (how you feel about yourself). For instance, if you don't believe that you are capable of earning more than a certain amount of money, you'll go from one position or career to another and find that in each case, you earn only as much as your expectations will allow.

Similarly, if you have relatively low self-esteem, you'll find that in one relationship after another, (both personally and in your career) you will tend to attract people who will put you down.

Let's look at some specific steps you can take to create new patterns that will improve every area of your life:

- **Identify your current patterns.** Take stock of the results you've produced in the following areas: your career, financial circumstances, health status, professional and personal relationships. Are you steadily advancing in your career ... or are you bouncing from job to job or stagnating in a position you hate? Do you feel that colleagues appreciate your efforts or are you regularly criticized "for no good reason"?

After identifying your patterns, ask yourself: *What beliefs do I have that contribute to these outcomes?* For instance, you may believe that "You can only earn money after a lot of struggle" ... or that "People will ultimately let you down." Make a list of *your* beliefs.

- **Stop placing the blame on others or on external circumstances.** If you've identified any patterns you don't like, the solution is not found in blaming your parents, your employer or your spouse. And, guess what? It won't help to blame yourself either! You'll just feel worse. Simply acknowledge the fact that you are perpetuating the pattern because of **your** thinking and **your** behavior.

- **Visualize the new pattern you wish to develop.** Your mind is now filled with pictures that support your *existing* circumstances! To break free from this, you must substitute images of what you *choose* to become. So, if you want to be more confident, imagine yourself acting with more assurance. For instance, you might think of yourself delivering an effective presentation in front of a large group in your company.

- **Watch your words.** Be very careful about what you say, both to yourself ("self-talk") and to others. Words and phrases that put you down or describe your limitations will keep you from establishing a new pattern.

- **Distance yourself from those who exhibit your "old" pattern.** If you want to break a dependency on drugs or alcohol, you can't continue to hang around people who abuse these substances, right? Similarly, if you want to break a chain of negative thinking, don't keep company with negative thinkers.

- **Take action that supports the new pattern.** For instance, those having financial problems might give up the idea of shopping around to save a few pennies on a gallon of milk. If you are *obsessed* with saving a few cents, the message you send to your mind is, "Money is scarce and a few cents is going to make a difference to me." If you truly believe that you are going to earn a considerable amount of money in the near future, those few cents would not concern you.

Start paying attention to recurring situations in your life. They aren't happening by "accident;" rather, they are a reflection of what's going on inside of you. When you elevate your thinking about what's possible — and feel good about yourself — you'll begin to produce miracles!

16

Life Lessons from Jason

Out of difficulties grow miracles.

—Jean de la Bruyere

You might have seen the amazing story that was shown on many television stations about Jason McElwain, the autistic teenager who performed miraculously when he got the chance to play in a high school basketball game. For those who are not familiar with this story, here is what happened.

In 2006, Jason was 17 years old and a student at Greece Athena High School in New York. He is autistic and served as manager of the school's basketball team. During the team's games, Jason sat on the bench, wearing a white shirt and black tie. Jim Johnson, the coach of the team, invited Jason to suit up in uniform for the team's final game of the season. He told Jason that he would try to put him into the game if Greece Athena was ahead by a sufficient number of points.

Well, Jason got into the game with four minutes left. After missing his first two shots, he hit 6 out of 10 three-point shots (shots taken from more than 20 feet) and scored 20 points. In the end, he was the game's leading scorer, although he played only four minutes! The crowd went wild and stormed onto the court to congratulate Jason and to celebrate his astonishing performance.

To be sure, Jason's story is inspirational and heart-warming. What's more, I think there are important lessons that we can all learn from this young man.

Jason demonstrated the power of attitude and enthusiasm. When Jason was asked about his job responsibilities as team manager, he explained that among other things, he sets the clock, keeps statistics and hands out water bottles and equipment. He also said that his job is "to be enthusiastic" and encourage the players. Isn't it interesting that he includes "to be enthusiastic" as part of his job description? Because Jason is so enthusiastic and supportive, the coach loves him. The players love him. Even the fans that night were shouting his name and rooting for him to get into the game.

The lesson here is that when you're energetic and positive, people **want** to be around you. They **want** to help you. If Jason had performed his responsibilities in a dull, listless manner, I don't think there's a chance that the coach would have considered letting him play in a game. Jason had given so much to the team that the coach wanted to reciprocate in some fashion. Perhaps, if we all add "to be enthusiastic" to our job descriptions, we'd have a lot more success at work and at home — and we'd gain a lot more cooperation from others.

Jason wasn't afraid to fail. Jason's first shot missed badly. He didn't even hit the rim. He also missed his second shot. Yet, he wasn't discouraged. Jason was going to keep on shooting. He then scored 20 points in a little more than three minutes! How many of us take a shot or two in life (for example, on a sales call or in a personal relationship), get a poor result and then quit? Had Jason done that, he wouldn't have accomplished his incredible feat. As with any endeavor, it often takes a little time before we get "in a groove" and things go our way. We have to be willing to endure the "misses" until we get on track.

Jason was willing to serve. Jason's first choice was not to be the team manager. He wanted to play basketball for the junior varsity team. He tried out but wasn't good enough. Instead of sulking and giving up on basketball, he willingly took the job as team manager of the varsity squad. He loves basketball and this was his opportunity to be around the game. So often, we don't reach our initial goal and we let our ego get in the way. We don't want to accept a lesser role or play "second fiddle," even temporarily.

Do what you love. Jason shows us that great opportunities often appear when you engage in activities that you're passionate about. Here's a guy who absolutely loves basketball. You can see it on his face when he's out on the court helping the other players or shooting around by himself. When you do what you love, you may make a lot of money; but then again, you may not. However, you will be happier and attract more positive experiences into your life — and perhaps even create a "miracle" as Jason has done.

Jason was prepared to seize the moment. Let's not forget that Jason practiced his shooting all the time. Although he didn't have game experience, he shot around in the gym on a regular basis. He knew he could make long shots, and when given the chance in a game, he made the majority of his shots. Let's turn to your dream. Are you ready for your opportunity? Have you done the practice, the research and whatever else is necessary for you to be ready to seize your moment? The time to prepare is now. If you wait until the opportunity arrives, it's too late.

Jason helped us to expand what we thought was possible. If someone had told you that an autistic teenager serving as a high school basketball team manager was put into an actual game, hit six out of 10 three point shots, and scored 20 points in just over three minutes, you'd say that could only happen in a movie. Yet this was real life. Not only that, but the President of the United States visited Jason at an airport near his home. Jason was interviewed on CBS-TV during the Final Four round of the 2006 NCAA basketball tournament. In addition, a documentary of his story was shown to millions of people around the world. Former basketball legend Magic Johnson came to the school gym to meet Jason and announce that a deal had been made to acquire the movie rights to Jason's story. Jason has achieved what many would say was "impossible," and yet we know deep down that we, too, have the ability to create magic in our own lives if we'll expand our view of what is possible.

Congratulations, Jason on your magnificent accomplishments — and for giving us a formula for successful living.

17

It's Time for Your Tune-Up

We know what we are, but know not what we may be.
— William Shakespeare

I f you own a car, you probably take it into the service station for maintenance at regular intervals. You want to make sure the engine is running smoothly. You want any worn parts to be replaced, or your tires to be safe and balanced. Often, the mechanic has a checklist of the items that need to be addressed. When you pick up your car after the service has been completed, you drive off with a vehicle in better shape to get back on the road and get you where you want to go.

Just as your car has needs that should be addressed regularly, you too can benefit by giving yourself a "tune-up." During your personal mental tune-up, you can examine the old routines that need to be replaced or identify new actions that will rev up your engine. Here is a checklist you can use for your tune-up:

Take a class or study a new subject. Learning something new will be exciting and will expose you to new people and new situations. Whether it's art history, ballroom dancing or learning a new language, this will rejuvenate you as you re-discover the joy of learning and broaden your horizons. Unlike your school days when subjects were "forced" upon you, now you can *choose* those subjects that are most appealing to you.

Stop participating in activities or organizations that no longer interest you. The fact that you joined an organization or have engaged in an activity does not mean that you enter into a lifetime contract to keep doing it until you die. Are there any organizations that you belong to that are no longer fun or interesting to you? Maybe you've outgrown an activity or group. After all, you're not the same person that you were 10 years ago. When you get some of this "dead wood" out of the way, you open up the way to new, more relevant activities.

Confront a fear that stands in the way of your personal or professional growth. Fear holds us back from reaching our potential and living an exciting life. We have dreams and goals, but we won't take steps toward them because of a variety of fears — the fear that we might fail, the fear that someone may criticize us, the fear of the unknown, or even the fear that we might succeed. When you face these fears head-on, you gain self-esteem and confidence. If you have trouble coming up with a fear to confront, tackle public speaking. Join a Toastmasters group in your area. You may be uncomfortable at the beginning, but you'll learn valuable skills and gain confidence, which will serve you well.

Examine whether your activities are in line with your stated priorities. Ask people about their priorities, and they'll probably tell you that it is their family, faith or their health. The only problem is that their activities are often completely at odds with what they're saying — e.g., they talk about wanting to live a healthy lifestyle, but you see them with a plate of nachos. What do **you** need to do to bring your activities in line with your priorities? If you will not make any changes to be more consistent, then don't kid yourself any longer. Your priorities are simply not what you say they are.

Take care of any "unfinished business." If you're holding a grudge or resentment against anyone, especially a close family member, let go of it immediately. This is draining your energy. If that other person leaves this earth without you having resolved the issue, you will regret it for the rest of your life. You don't have to approve of what the other person did to you. You don't have to spend time with the other person. Furthermore, it's irrelevant if the other person still disagrees with you, or even hates you. You simply need to release the resentment and move on.

Support others in the pursuit of their dreams. Take every opportunity to support friends, relatives or colleagues who are pursuing their dreams. From your own personal experience, you know how tough it is to blaze a new trail, start a new business or try to achieve something very ambitious. You needed all the help and support you could get. Give that support to others. It will make a world of difference to them. In addition, getting involved in their dreams will rekindle your enthusiasm and encourage you to pursue your own dreams.

Do something to improve your health and energy. Start treating your health as a top priority, instead of something you "don't have time for." If you don't have time to maintain your car, or if you put sludge into the gas tank, your car sputters or breaks down. The same holds true for you. Find the time to walk several times each week or to do some other type of exercise at home or in the gym. As a result, you're going to feel better and perform more effectively ... on the job and at home.

In addition, taking care of your body builds self-esteem. This isn't about becoming a tri-athlete or a bodybuilder. It's about attaining a level of basic fitness. Energy is a vital ingredient for living a successful, productive life. Isn't it interesting that you take your children for all of their doctor visits and make sure that they are physically active, yet you don't take the same care of yourself? Don't wait another day to start a fitness regimen that will preserve your health and vitality.

Have you gone through the checklist for your tune-up and are you ready to attend to each of these items? You wouldn't want your mechanic to skip over any areas when tending to your car. So, don't cheat yourself by ignoring these areas. When you give yourself this regular tune-up, your body, mind and spirit will be firing on all cylinders.

18

Avoid These
"Communication Killers"

*Most conversations are simply monologues
delivered in the presence of a witness.*

— *Margaret Miller*

In both our personal and business lives, there are times
when we connect with other people and make them
happy to communicate with us. In these instances,
there is a free flow of information where both parties leave
the communication with positive feelings. Then, of course,
there are times when obstacles get in the way of effective
communication, and we leave with a mediocre or negative
impression about what just took place.

To a large extent, your success as a communicator is a
result of certain strategies that you may be employing, either
consciously or without much thought.

There's a lot at stake when you communicate. If you want
positive personal relationships or a successful marriage, the
effectiveness of your communication will likely determine
the type of person you attract as well as the fulfillment you
get from your marriage. In business, the effective communicators are the ones who will be respected and promoted to

leadership positions. In sales, good communicators are more persuasive, establish rapport and sell more than those with weak skills.

To be effective, it's imperative to follow sound communication strategies. However, even the most skilled among us sometimes communicate in ways that turn people off. Here, then, are some communication "killers" to watch out for. By avoiding these traps, we can build rapport, leave a positive impression on others, and make communicating with us a valuable experience.

1. **Making the other person "wrong."** Too many people view communication as an argument, where the objective is to prove that they are "right" and that the other person is wrong. The other person will always resent your attempt to establish that he or she is wrong. Think about it: how do YOU like it when someone tries to prove that you are wrong? I'll bet that you resent when a co-worker or family member plays this game with you. Many times we assert that we are right in matters of opinion, where there really is no right or wrong. Even if you are quoting a statistic and you know the other person is mistaken, you gain little by insisting that he or she is wrong. Granted, there are some instances where it is important to point out another person's error — such as when someone insists the meeting is on Monday and you know it is on Tuesday. However, this is the exception and it's far better to make your point without setting up winners and losers.

2. **Talking too much about yourself.** Just about everyone falls into this trap. You get in a discussion with someone and you dominate the conversation by talking about yourself, while allowing the other party very little opportunity to speak. When you talk only about yourself without letting the other party participate,

you give the message that you don't care about the other person. This creates resentment and that person will not look forward to communicating with you in the future. On the other hand, when you listen to someone else, that individual feels validated and important. In your upcoming conversations, make a note of the percentage of time you are speaking, as opposed to listening. Remember this illustration: we are born with two ears and one mouth, and should strive to use them in that proportion. When you listen twice as much as you speak, the other person will have a positive impression of you and will often feel that you are an interesting conversationalist, even though you did very little talking.

3. **Interrupting**. This is one of the most common communications blunders. We start out listening to someone but then we begin to think of what we're going to say next and we tune them out. When we have our thoughts ready to launch, we break into the discussion and start talking. This is insulting to the other party as you did not let that person complete his or her comments. Discipline yourself to let others finish their thoughts before you chime in with yours.

4. **Changing the subject abruptly in a group discussion**. This is a variation on interrupting. You're talking about your recent vacation with a group of friends when someone cuts you off and says something like, "Did you see the baseball game last night?" How does that make you feel? In most cases, the person cutting you off wants to steer the discussion back to a topic where he or she can re-assume command of the discussion and dominate once again. Sometimes, the person who cut you off just has a limited attention span and needs to keep changing subjects. Regardless of the motive, it's rude.

5. **Talking too much about the negative**. People are bombarded with negative news from the media. Terrorism, violent crime and natural disasters are just a few of the topics that receive many hours of daily coverage. Then there's the negative "drama" in your personal life—your disappointing relationships, unfulfilling career, bouts with illness. While it's only natural to share your life experiences with others, especially friends and co-workers, you don't need to tell them everything that's wrong. What makes you think they want to hear about your dysfunctional family or the fact that you're not appreciated at work? People have enough troubles of their own without hearing your tales of woe! Keep your conversations uplifting and others will look forward to speaking with you.

6. **Treating your technology device as more important than the person you're speaking to**. Here's a problem that's growing way out of control. More and more people feel the need to be "connected" with the world 24/7. These individuals are slaves to their cell phones and hand held computers. It doesn't matter whether you're in the middle of a conversation or meeting with them. If their phone rings or their device shows a message coming in, they immediately divert their attention away from you. The message they're giving is that the incoming communication is more important than anything you have to offer. Unless you are expecting an emergency message (which is rarely the case), turn off the phones and hand-held devices when meeting with others. You'll have plenty of time to examine those messages later.

7. **Looking for more "important" people**. This usually happens at networking events. You're engaged in a discussion with someone when you see a person you perceive as "more important" than the person

you're currently talking to. Your eyes dart toward the "important" person and all you want to do is break away from the existing discussion and approach the person you perceive as more valuable. This is an insult to the person you're talking to. If you feel you must interrupt the conversation to seize an opportunity to speak to someone else, explain the situation and promise the person that you will be back to resume your conversation with him or her. Then make sure to get back to that person after your other discussion is complete.

You might argue that there are many successful people who commit these communications blunders. I'd agree with you on that point. However those people are making enemies needlessly by their rudeness. They would enjoy even more respect and success if they revised their communication strategies.

In the ensuing days, weeks and months, keep this list of communications reminders in your wallet, purse, or on your desk. These are not simple habits to break and you'll need to be vigilant. Become a more effective communicator and watch as other people respect you more — and help you to get what you want.

19

The Tiny Black Dot

*The secret of happiness is to count your blessings
while others are adding up their troubles.*

— William Penn

During some of my presentations, I take an 8 ½ x 11 piece of white paper and make a little black dot in the middle. Then I show the sheet to people in the audience and ask them what they see. The majority will say that they see a black dot. Very few, if any, will tell me that they see a white sheet of paper with a tiny black dot.

We tend to look at our lives in very much the same way. We have our health, enough food to eat, a job that pays the bills and allows us some leisure activities, but we don't focus on that. We don't appreciate that. Instead, we concentrate on the tiny black dot — the 10% in our lives that we don't like ... or the things we wish we could change. By concentrating on the 10% that represents our problems or things we don't like, we develop a negative attitude and feel lousy. Plus, there's a universal principle that comes into play: we attract what we think about most. By focusing on what is lacking in our lives, we create more experiences of scarcity.

Think about your life. Are you paying too much attention to the 10% that isn't what you want it to be ... as opposed to the 90% that's going well? I'm not saying we should ignore our challenges or things we'd like to change. But if we paid a lot more attention to the 90% that IS working, we'd have a better attitude and we'd get better results.

When it comes to your job, do you concentrate on all the positive aspects of your position, or do you gripe about your salary and your co-workers, or the fact that someone else got the promotion you wanted?

What about the basic necessities of life? Do you feel gratitude every day for the food you eat, the clothing you have, the roof above your head ... or do you take all of these things for granted?

And let's not forget your body and your health. How much time do you spend thinking about what IS working? Your body is a miracle, make no mistake about that. There's nothing "ho-hum" about your body and its day to day operation. Albert Einstein once said that there are two ways to live your life — one way is as though nothing is a miracle ... the other is as though everything is a miracle. Most of us walk around with a ho-hum attitude about the miracle of our bodies. We treat this amazing creation as if it's no big deal.

Consider this: your heart is only the size of a fist and yet it pumps blood through your body. Every day, the heart pumps about 2,000 gallons of blood and beats about 100,000 times. That's just in one day. In one year, that amounts to 36,500,000 beats. And in most cases, the heart just keeps on beating 36,500,000 times a year for many decades. Stop for a moment and recognize the enormity of this miracle. And, of course, you don't have to change any body parts or beat your chest manually to keep your heart going. It automatically beats and sends the blood through your body with no effort on your part.

Now, let's consider your brain. The brain and spinal cord are made up of many cells, which include neurons. There are about 100 billion neurons in the brain. 100 billion! Neurons are nerve cells that transmit nerve signals to and from the brain at up to 200 miles per hour. Isn't this amazing?

Of course, your ears ... your eyes ... well, I could go on all day about the miracle of your body and how we take it for granted. Just one final example to drive the point home.

When you get a cold and have difficulty breathing for a few days, I bet you'll often tell everyone that you are congested and don't feel well. When the cold clears up in a week and your breathing returns to normal, you probably *don't* say: "My breathing is perfect today! I'm able to get all the oxygen I need!" Why does it make sense to complain about your breathing for the one week it is impaired ... while failing to acknowledge the other 51 weeks when your breathing is full and healthy?

Stop taking this incredible body for granted. Appreciate all the things that ARE working! You're a walking miracle, and part of an extraordinary universe.

Some of you may feel that ignoring the black dot is not the answer — and that you need to focus on the black dot to improve certain conditions in your life. Well, if you choose this route, here are three strategies you could use:

1. Worry about the black dot.

2. Complain about the black dot.

3. Take some proactive steps to eliminate or reduce the black dot.

The only strategy that makes sense is #3. Yet many people select strategies #1 and #2, which only makes them more miserable.

Be brutally honest with yourself. Are there any areas of your life where you're ignoring the large white sheet and seeing only the tiny black dot? Do you see the faults of those at work or at home, and seldom affirm people for their positive contributions to your life? If you're like most of us, you have an abundance of blessings, yet you're often blind to them.

If you've been staring at some tiny black dots recently, take responsibility for that. And recognize that nobody is forcing you to *keep* your eyes on the black dot. You've developed the habit of focusing on the negative and your life (and the lives of those around you) will be greatly enriched if you start to shift your vision toward the white sheet.

You have a choice. You can keep staring at the black dot and telling others about all the things that are wrong in your life, or you can begin to appreciate your many blessings. Sounds like a pretty easy choice to make, doesn't it?

20

How to Enter a New World

Your world is a living expression
of how you are using and have used your mind.

— Earl Nightingale

During my presentations, I often pose this question to the audience: "Over the course of your life, how many of you went from having a relatively low level of self-esteem to having a much higher level of self-esteem?" In a group of 100 people, about 10 people will raise their hands.

I then ask those 10 people, "When you changed your feelings about yourself, how many of you found that you attracted very different people and very different circumstances into your life?" Inevitably, all 10 hands go up. When I invite them to explain what happened after they increased their feelings of self-worth, they tell remarkable, inspiring stories about the positive changes in their lives. Some will explain how they advanced in their careers. Others will proudly describe how their relationships improved or they met a wonderful person who they later married. Listening to their stories, you'd think that these people were dropped into a new world, one they never inhabited before.

Before I continue, a definition of self-esteem would seem helpful. A simple definition is that self-esteem is the degree to which you like and value yourself. One of the best definitions I've seen was offered by Nathaniel Branden, author of *The Six Pillars of Self-Esteem*. He defines self-esteem as "the disposition to experience oneself as competent to cope with the basic challenges of life and as worthy of happiness."

Let's get back to the stories told by my audience members. What explains the changes that take place in their lives? What we're seeing is the Law of Attraction at work, or the principle that "like attracts like." You attract into your life what you habitually dwell upon and what you feel you deserve. Your inner thoughts and feelings are projected outward and, like a magnet, you attract conditions that are in accord with those thoughts and feelings.

Now, I'll admit that I can't show you precisely how the Law of Attraction operates. It isn't visible to the eye. It's working "behind the scenes" but it is very real nevertheless. Here's an analogy that may help to explain this principle — the stations on your radio. Assume there are 10 radio stations that you can tune into. Stations 1-3 are for those with low self-esteem; Stations 4-6 are for those with self-esteem in the middle range; and Stations 7-10 are reserved for those who feel good about themselves. This is an oversimplification, to be sure, but stay with me.

Let's assume further that your life is "playing" on Station 5. Your self-esteem is in the middle range. You'll find that the vast majority of the people you attract are on Stations 4-6. Thus, you're interacting with people who are on a similar "frequency." Occasionally, you will encounter some people from other stations. However, you will not feel comfortable spending much time with those on Station 2 — nor will you feel that you fit in with those on Station 8.

It all comes down to what you think you deserve. You then attract the people and circumstances to confirm your feelings of self-worth.

The choice of who to attract is made below the surface — at the level of the subconscious mind. Consciously, nobody says "I want to attract people who will not treat me well or who won't appreciate me." However, at the subconscious level, they feel this is what they deserve. These feelings and beliefs are often formed in childhood. Often we re-create the relationships our parents experienced.

Think about your intimate relationships throughout your life. Think about your relationships at work. Do you see any similarities with the relationships your parents experienced in their lives? The example of your parents can be deeply embedded within your mind, whether you realize it or not. It's true that some people will create relationships and experiences that are the opposite of their parents, but this is more the exception.

Moving Forward

The concept of entering a new world and reaching the next level is not limited to those who feel they have low or mediocre self-esteem. It is also available to those with high self-esteem. After all, you can always develop a higher level of self-esteem and when you do, the circumstances in your life will improve dramatically. It just gets better and better!

How can you raise your level of self-esteem so you can take advantage of the Law of Attraction? Here are some techniques you might find helpful:

Take responsibility for the people and circumstances you have attracted thus far. If you continue to believe that forces outside of you are responsible for your relationships and your circumstances, you'll remain stuck. Once you accept that YOU are the cause of your present situation, you'll make different choices moving forward, which will attract new people and new conditions.

Stretch beyond your comfort zone. Self-esteem is not developed by simply standing in front of a mirror and saying "I love myself." As Nathaniel Branden's definition suggests, there is an element of competency to self-esteem. You must engage life and feel capable. When you sit on the sidelines and refuse to explore the limits of your potential, you feel stifled. You know there is more you can experience in life, and yet you're backing away. This lowers your self-esteem. Jump start your self-esteem by challenging yourself to move beyond the familiar. Learn a new skill. Take a public speaking class. Apply for a position in your organization that you've always wanted but were afraid to pursue. It doesn't matter whether you're successful. You will raise your self-esteem immediately by "getting in the game."

Change your vocabulary. You can't have high self-esteem when you continually put yourself down. What you say about yourself matters. For instance, from now on, whenever someone pays you a compliment, respond by saying "Thank you." If you reject the compliment, as many people do—"oh, it was nothing," they say—you're telling yourself that you don't deserve the praise and you'll attract people to confirm your low feelings of self-worth.

Respect yourself. Until you respect yourself, nobody else will respect you. Thus, when someone makes a verbally abusive comment to you or puts you down, make it clear that you won't accept that kind of language. You don't have to argue or prove that the other person is "wrong." As you show more and more respect for yourself, you will find that you don't attract abusive people into your life anymore. You're operating on a higher "frequency" and you now attract others who will value you instead of criticizing you. It's the Law of Attraction at work!

We're all human magnets, and our thoughts and feelings attract certain people and circumstances into our lives. As you value yourself more, you'll enter a new world of possibility. Exciting times lie ahead!

21

Big Setbacks, Big Victories

Everything flows out and in; everything has its tides; all things rise and fall; the pendulum-swing manifests in everything; the measure of the swing to the right, is the measure of the swing to the left.

— The Kybalion

Napoleon Hill, author of *Think and Grow Rich*, interviewed hundreds of the most successful people in the early 1900s, including Henry Ford, Thomas Edison and Andrew Carnegie. After conducting these extensive interviews, Hill observed that the greatest successes of many of these individuals came on the heels of their greatest failures and disappointments. Interesting, isn't it?

Of course, the principle works the other way as well. If you have a victory, you can expect to experience a corresponding setback or difficulty. For purposes of this article, we're going to focus on the seemingly negative events that precede victories.

In an ancient text known as The Kybalion, there is a discussion of The Law of Rhythm, which includes the metaphor of the pendulum. The pendulum swings to the left, and then the pendulum swings to the right. This applies to all of our life experiences and moods. According to this notion, those who experience large DOWNS will eventually experience large UPS.

Let's begin by looking at some examples from the world of athletics. Consider the road that the Boston Red Sox traveled to win the 2004 World Series. The Red Sox had not won a world championship in 86 years and had suffered several agonizing World Series defeats during that long stretch. To get into the 2004 World Series, the Red Sox had to defeat the Yankees in a best of seven game series. To make matters worse, their best pitcher, Curt Schilling, sustained a serious foot injury right before the series began.

The Yankees won the first three games of the series. The Yankees won Game 3 by the lopsided score of 19-8 and everyone wrote off the Red Sox at that point. Talk about being in a hole! In the history of postseason baseball, 25 teams had faced this situation, trailing 3-0. None of them had been able to win four straight games.

The Red Sox won two games in a row in Boston, bringing the series to 3-2. Then they came to New York to play the last two games in Yankee Stadium. Miraculously, the Red Sox won the two games in New York, winning the series 4-3. They went on to beat the Cardinals four straight games to capture the World Series. Most teams — and most individuals — quit when they face difficulties like the Red Sox faced. But the Red Sox hung in and turned some huge setbacks into a never-to-be-forgotten triumph.

Another example from the world of sports is gymnast Mary Lou Retton. After training with great discipline for years leading up to the 1984 Olympics, Mary Lou suffered a knee injury just six weeks before the Olympics. She had broken cartilage in her knee and needed surgery. The doctor told her she couldn't compete in the Olympics — that she would need to rehab the knee for 3 months. Mary Lou would not accept the doctor's prediction and would not give up on a dream she had worked so hard to achieve. She completed the rehabilitation in 3 weeks — instead of 3 months — and went on to win 5 Olympic medals, including an individual gold medal. Life tested Mary Lou by throwing her a big setback at the last moment. But because of her magnificent attitude and faith, she overcame that obstacle to become an Olympic champion.

Another great athlete, Lance Armstrong, was diagnosed with cancer in 1996 and was given a 50% chance of surviving. As you may know, he won seven consecutive Tour de France championships. From the brink of death ... to one of the most impressive accomplishments in sports history. The pendulum sure took a big swing in the opposite direction in Lance's life!

Naturally, this principle isn't limited to sports. When I think about someone who turned a huge setback into an extraordinary victory, Candace Lightner comes to mind. In 1980 in California, Candace learned that her 13-year old daughter was killed by a drunk driver, who struck the girl from behind on the sidewalk. To make matters worse, the driver was a repeat offender, who was out on bail..

It's hard to imagine anything more tragic than losing your child this way. Who could blame Candace if she retreated from life and became very negative? But that's not what she did. Just four months after the death of her daughter, Candace and a group of women in California created an organization called MADD — Mothers Against Drunk Driving. I'll bet you're very familiar with MADD. This group has had a phenomenal impact in changing laws on drunk driving and educating people and raising awareness about drunk driving. Once again, a crushing setback laid the groundwork for a stunning victory.

You don't have to form a national organization or become a celebrity to activate this principle. It's at work in *your* life all the time. Furthermore, the concept isn't limited to monumental setbacks and disappointments. The degree to which the pendulum swings one way will lead to a corresponding swing of the pendulum the opposite way.

Let me bring it a little closer to home. Have you ever had a job where you were fired or downsized — and then went on to find a better job...or started your own business? Ever have a relationship with someone that ended — and you were devastated. And you went on to a better relationship? And how about this one — you look for a house or apartment and you find what you think is the house or apartment of your dreams. You're incredibly excited. And then somehow the deal fell through and you didn't get it. Then something else comes along — another place — and it's even better than the original dream house! You're so glad that the first deal fell through. In each case, a setback preceded a positive outcome.

When you suffer a setback in your life, it's only natural to feel frustrated and disappointed. But don't let the setbacks destroy your attitude and don't give up. Remember that difficulties precede victories. Get excited about the possibilities that are in store when the pendulum swings back the other way.

22

Start Shoveling!

Once you're moving, you can keep moving.
— Ronald Alan Weiss

Shortly after my wife and I moved into our house, there was a large snowfall on the East Coast that left about 30 inches of snow on our front walkway. The path is about 35 feet, and when I first went out to survey the situation, the task of shoveling it seemed monumental. I immediately thought, "This is going to take forever!"

I stood there for about 30 seconds looking at what I had to do, feeling more than a bit discouraged. Then, I picked up my shovel and started digging into the snow. I was moving at a pretty good clip and fortunately, the snow was fairly soft. About ten minutes later, I took a short break and noticed that I had made a significant dent in the job. I could actually see significant progress, which gave me the momentum to get right back at it.

About 30 minutes into the job, I had completed almost half of the walkway. I also surveyed what was left to do, but unlike 30 minutes ago, I could now see the end in sight. This further motivated me to keep shoveling vigorously. About one hour into the job, I had completed the entire walkway! I felt a tremendous surge of energy and was ready to shovel some more. You've probably felt a similar exhilaration after completing a major project. In the end, however, I decided that I had done enough and took a well-deserved rest.

After sitting inside for a few minutes, I realized that the shoveling project had a lot to teach me about the path to achieving our objectives and realizing our cherished dreams.

Most importantly, I realized the importance of starting any project with a head of steam. I'm not a big believer in the often-used phrase, "beginning is winning." In my experience, *persevering* is winning. However, beginning **is** the crucial first step if you want to achieve any goal or explore new avenues. It's so important to start energetically, because you can look up after a relatively short period of time and see progress. That gives you the momentum to keep moving forward.

This isn't to suggest that you should avoid planning and rush into your project with wild abandon. Definitely do your research. But when you do begin, leave the starting blocks strongly and quickly. It's a lot more effective than dipping your toe in the water. When you dive into the water, you feel exhilarated and you're already in motion. When you stick your toe in, you hesitate and tend to remain stationery for long periods of time.

Of course, the worst thing you can do is to keep talking about what you're going to do, while taking no action. Sadly, this is the approach many people take. They are caught in the trap of "Someday, I'll ...." You know how that goes:

Someday, I'll begin the exercise program ...
Someday, I'll take a trip to Hawaii ...
Someday, I'll go back to school to get my degree ...
Someday, I'll write a book ...
Someday, I'll do some acting or singing ...

"Someday, I'll ..." drains your energy and keeps you stuck. How much more effective to pick up the shovel and start shoveling! Thus, instead of talking about exercising, you start exercising. Instead of talking about going back to school, you register for classes. Instead of talking about writing a book, you sit at your computer, develop an outline and start writing.

When you pick up the shovel and start shoveling as soon as you can, you get another benefit. You achieve your objective in less time than you initially thought was possible. Let's say you want to take a trip to Hawaii "some day." You may have had this desire for years. Each time the thought enters your mind, you dwell on all the obstacles in your way. You don't have the time. You don't have the money. So, you file the thought away, hoping you can take the trip "some day."

Here's a better way to make sure you take that trip to Hawaii — and sooner than you think. Today, start investigating the Hawaiian trip as if you were going to be traveling there immediately. Find out the airlines that go there. Check out the air fares, including any special discounts being offered. Go online and check out the hotels or places you could rent during your visit. While online, you could look at pictures of Hawaii and learn all about the islands, which would get you even more excited. You're shoveling fast and furious now!

Several things will happen as a result of your shoveling. You may find that the trip is more affordable than you originally thought. Or, you might be so excited that you will find a way to earn the extra money you need to pay for the trip. You might even open a "vacation account" at the bank and start putting away funds to make your dream come true. You see, you're now actively thinking about Hawaii and the ways to make the vacation possible — instead of thinking about all the obstacles in your way.

When you start shoveling, you become actively engaged in creating the result you want. You generate enthusiasm and momentum. You might face roadblocks, but you're able to get around them.

Many of us don't pick up the shovel because we fear that we're not ready to go after our dream. We want everything to line up in perfect order so we'll have a clear path, with no unexpected detours, no criticism and no disappointments. You'll rarely find any situation with perfect conditions. That's just an excuse for never starting. When your heart and mind are actively engaged and you're on fire about achieving something, you are simultaneously directing your subconscious mind to find out a way to get it for you. And the subconscious mind will get the job done for you, usually in miraculous ways.

So, are there any goals or dreams where you have been delaying or failing to take action? If so, put on your boots, dig in and start shoveling ... today!

23

Anatomy of a Miracle

Whatever you can do or dream you can, begin it.
Boldness has genius, power and magic in it!

— Johann Wolfgang Von Goethe

As the final seconds of the game ticked down, millions of people around the world couldn't believe what was about to happen. And as the game ended, we heard broadcaster Al Michaels' now famous words, "Do you believe in miracles?"

A miracle it was. The greatest upset in sports history. Yes, I'm referring to the 1980 U.S. Olympic Hockey Team victory over the Soviet Union in Lake Placid, New York. The American squad went on to capture the gold medal that year.

Let's remember what the American team was up against — and why this victory against the Soviets was truly a "miracle." Going into the 1980 Olympic games, the powerful, professional Soviet hockey team had won four consecutive gold medals and was undefeated in the Olympics since 1968. In 1979, the Soviets beat the professional National Hockey League All-Stars 6-0.

The U.S. team, on the other hand, was a collection of untested college players. Shortly before the 1980 Olympics, the Soviets played the U.S. Olympic Team in an exhibition and the Soviets embarrassed the U.S. squad by a score of 10-3. Everyone knew there was no way these college players could even compete with the Soviets, let alone beat them. Everyone that is, except Herb Brooks, who coached the 1980 U.S. team.

Brooks thought that he could pull off a miracle. He believed the U.S. could win a gold medal, even if it required beating the "unbeatable" Soviet team. In 2004, Walt Disney Pictures released a movie about Coach Brooks and the 1980 U.S. Olympic team, aptly titled "Miracle." It's a wonderful, inspiring movie starring Kurt Russell as Coach Brooks. After watching the movie recently, I couldn't help observing that while every miracle is unique, there are some elements that most miracles have in common. For instance:

A miracle is the result of a BIG dream. It's hard to imagine a dream that was bolder or more audacious than that of Herb Brooks. How on earth could he even fathom that he could mold a bunch of college hockey players into a team that would defeat the mighty Soviets? Remember, the Soviet team was thought to be invincible. Yet Brooks allowed himself to dream that he could coach a team that would defeat this powerhouse.

You see, many people dream too small and then they can't get excited about the pursuit of the dream. It's the big dream that gets your blood moving and it's the big dream that gets other people excited about joining you in the quest.

People often wonder, "How do I know if I should pursue my dream, or whether it's simply "unrealistic?" Richard Bach said, "You're never given a wish without also being given the power to make it come true." So, if your dream is constantly "speaking" to you and there's tremendous emotion attached to the dream, that's a positive sign. Then again, if you would like to accomplish something but it doesn't send chills down your spine thinking about it, there's a good chance that you're really not energized about that goal and you won't be willing to do what it takes to turn the dream into reality.

A miracle is not achieved by talent alone. There's a great line in the movie where Coach Brooks tells his players, "You don't have enough talent to win on talent." There was no denying that the Soviet team had more talent than the American youngsters. Brooks knew, however, that the team with the greatest talent doesn't always win. When selecting the team from the hundreds of college hockey players who tried out, Brooks surprised people when he cut many talented players. Instead, he chose players who did not have as much skill but fit within his unique system and had the psychological makeup he desired.

A miracle requires creative thinking. Other teams in North America had attempted to defeat the Soviets by playing a "North American style" of hockey. What Brooks realized is that this style of play was not working! In other words, the Soviets were able to win against that strategy time after time. Brooks determined that he would use a different strategy, abandoning the traditional North American style. He was willing to innovate, to develop a new system that stressed superior conditioning, discipline and speed. He knew it would be challenging for his players to learn and execute … but his willingness to innovate eventually paid off with a gold medal.

A miracle requires uncommon sacrifice. Nobody said that a miracle comes easily. Herb Brooks warned his players that they would have to be "uncommon" men to defeat the Soviets and win a gold medal. They would have to develop a superior level of conditioning. His practice sessions were excruciating. The most memorable scene of the movie takes place during one of the exhibition games the team played preparing for the Olympics. The U.S. Team had not given a full effort, and when the game ended, Brooks called his already tired players out on the ice and made them skate "sprints" up and down the ice. He wouldn't stop even when the lights in the rink were shut off! His message: if we want to achieve a miracle, we must give it our all in every second of every game.

A miracle is generally a team effort. When you set out to achieve a miracle, you're fooling yourself if you think you can do it on your own. Extraordinary achievements require a collection of individuals pulling together for a common goal. Brooks assembled a group that played as a team, with their individual egos in check.

A miracle is often inspired by adversity. Herb Brooks was an excellent hockey player in his younger days. In 1960, he tried out for the U.S. Olympic hockey team and he was the very last person to be cut from the squad. That team went on to win a gold medal. Can you imagine the disappointment he must have felt as he saw himself lose out on a gold medal as a player? He was motivated by this setback to get that gold medal as a coach.

It's easy to think that miracles are for "other people" — the people we see on TV or read about in the newspaper. And yet a part of us knows that we, too, can perform miracles. Rekindle your ability to perform extraordinary feats by renting the movie, "Miracle." (the DVD version includes an interview with Herb Brooks, who tragically died in a car accident before the movie was released.)

I can't say for sure, but I'll bet that whatever you want to achieve is not as monumental as what Herb Brooks set out to do in the 1980 Olympics. Perhaps it's time for you to embark on a bold dream, using your own innovative approach and a willingness to persist through all the obstacles. Then, one day, maybe we'll be watching the movie of YOUR miracle!

24

The Million Dollar Reward

Always do more than is required of you.
— George F. Patton

A client in Africa ordered some of our motivational resources and sent us a check drawn on a bank in New York. I went to my bank to deposit the check.

As I walked into the branch that morning, I saw the person who handles the business accounts. Let's call her Jane. Before depositing the check, I showed it to Jane, just to make sure there would be no delay in getting the funds credited to my account. She assured me that everything looked fine and that the check should promptly be paid by the financial institution in New York.

I thought nothing more of it until I was checking my mail about 6 days later — and saw an envelope from my bank. Inside there was a COPY of the check from our African client with a notation that the check was returned "unpaid."

A day or two later, I went to my branch and spoke with Jane. She looked at the copy of the check and couldn't understand why it had been returned unpaid, nor could she explain what happened to the original check. She promised to look into it and get back to me later that same day. I didn't hear from Jane that day, so I called her the following day. She said that she contacted the bank in New York but hadn't heard back yet.

About three days later, I called Jane and she told me she was still working on it but hadn't gotten an answer yet from the New York bank. Three more **weeks** passed and I went back to my bank. Jane had not come up with any answer but assured me she was diligently working on it.

Admittedly, I was losing patience. Exasperated, I looked at Jane and said, *"If there was a one million dollar reward if the bank could find out within 24 hours why that check was returned unpaid, I believe the bank would immediately find the answer and be able to claim the reward."*

Jane assured me that she would continue to follow up. One thing is for sure. Jane did not have the "million dollar reward" mindset. She was content to make a call here and there and then passively wait for a response. If she had the million dollar reward approach, I believe, without question, she could have solved the issue in a few hours at most.

In case you're wondering, the story has a happy ending (at least for me!). My client in Africa became aware that the check had not been paid. The President of the company was kind enough to contact his bank in Africa and asked them to find out what happened. Within one day, I had the answer.

My bank had lost the original check and had sent a photocopy to the bank in New York. The New York bank rejected the copy because my bank had failed to include a statement that the original had been lost. When my bank provided a statement to that effect, the check was immediately paid and the funds credited to my account.

Isn't it interesting that a few people in Africa with a million dollar reward mindset were able to solve the riddle in one day, whereas my bank — located in the same state where the check was forwarded — could not find out in one month?

Don't get me wrong. Jane is a very nice person. But she didn't have the million dollar reward mentality. As a result, she rendered inferior service to the bank's clients.

We've all dealt with individuals or companies who work with a million dollar reward mindset. They go the extra mile and act with a sense of urgency. They don't let circumstances or others dictate the quality of service they render. They make things happen as soon as they can. They take a personal interest in each client, regardless of the amount involved.

Take a look at the way you do your work. Do you act as if a million dollar reward was riding on your performance? Do you render the service in a way you'd like to be treated if you were the client?

When you get right down to it, the million dollar reward mentality is an "attitude." It's the way you approach your work. You can go the extra mile and serve others with a sense of urgency ... or you can shuffle papers, make a few calls and let things happen.

Never forget that the million dollar reward mindset is not just about helping others. It's about helping yourself. In the workplace, you can spot the people with the million dollar reward attitude a mile away. They're the individuals who will advance and be rewarded over the long haul.

I'm not advocating that you work at warp speed and rush around in a frenzy. This isn't about speed. And, of course, some items will have a higher priority than others. What this is really about is *caring* ... caring about your clients ... caring about the quality of your work ... and caring enough to work hard to make sure that others are taken care of.

Do yourself, your co-workers and your clients a favor. When you have a task to do, make believe there's a million dollar reward riding on your performance. And before you say you can't do something, ask yourself this question: if there was a million dollar reward to complete this task, could I do it? You just may surprise yourself about what is possible.

25

Be Unrealistic!

You are never given a wish without also
being given the power to make it come true.

— Richard Bach

Whenever you're doing work for which you are very well-suited, it's likely that some BIG goals are going to pop into your mind — grand ideas with huge payoffs that will benefit you and (hopefully) many others as well. If you're like most people, however, it's equally likely that a little voice inside your head will immediately dismiss these goals as crazy, outrageous and, of course, *unrealistic!* After all, how could *you* possibly hope to accomplish such incredible outcomes?

Let's take a closer look at this word, "unrealistic." Was it realistic, in the early 1960s, for John F. Kennedy to proclaim that we would put a man on the moon by the end of that decade? In 1990, was it realistic to believe that millions of people worldwide would be exchanging e-mail messages every day? Was it ever realistic to believe that a sheep could be cloned?

As you'll probably admit, all of these things were at one time unrealistic. And yet, all of them were accomplished! Why? Because certain people dared to "dream big" and took the steps necessary to bring their visions into reality. Take a moment to think about it. Are there any goals that you have given up on ... or hesitate to pursue ... because you decided they were "unrealistic?"

Allow me to share some of my own experiences. Twenty years ago, when I was feeling depressed and very unhappy in my career as an attorney (and with no understanding of self-development concepts), it was unrealistic that I would be going around the country to speak to audiences about attitude and motivation. It was unrealistic that thousands of people each year would be listening to my audio programs or reading my articles about leading a happier, more successful life. Simply put, if you told me, 20 years ago, that I'd be doing what I'm now doing, I would have said that you were out of your mind!

Please understand that I point these things out not to give myself a pat on the back, but rather to emphasize just how "unrealistic" my own journey has been. You, too, can accomplish some astounding, "unrealistic" goals in your life, and here are some ideas that will assist you in bringing your dreams into reality:

1. **You wouldn't have the dream unless you could implement it.** Reread the Richard Bach quote at the beginning of this article. The universe does not waste its efforts by giving you the desire to accomplish something ... unless you also have the potential to achieve it. Now, no one said it would be easy! Your goal may take years to attain, and there may be numerous setbacks — before you can claim victory.

2. **A positive attitude is the foundation.** You can achieve something extraordinary only if you have a dynamic positive attitude and a strong belief in yourself and your abilities.

3. **Don't expect others to feel and see your vision.** You may be able to picture your outcome in vivid detail.

This is *your* personal vision — so don't be discouraged when you find that others (even those close to you) can't "tune into" that dream. All that counts is that *you* see it ... and feel it. Make sure to stay away from negative people who will tell you that you are being foolish and that you will fail. You don't need the approval of these people.

4. **Enthusiasm is crucial.** Bold objectives are achieved by those who are "on fire" about accomplishing them. So, are you excited about your goal? When you are speaking about that topic to others, can they sense your passion? If you are lukewarm about achieving your goal or are just in it for the money, you probably won't succeed. Also, if you are trying to achieve a goal that someone else has set for you — but your heart isn't in — you will face disappointment.

5. **Commitment gets the job done.** Sure, many people are excited at the outset. But, they quickly lose interest when obstacles appear in their path. And, with any "unrealistic" goal, you can bet that the trip won't be all fun and games. You're going to face some tough times on the way to your goal. Those who are committed have decided that they are in it for the long haul — *however long that haul may take.* They usually have a timetable for realizing their dream, but quitting is simply not an option. That's the mindset that achieves the "impossible."

6. **Your everyday progress will look quite ordinary.** When you look back at the accomplishment of most "unrealistic" goals, you're going to find that they were achieved by harnessing the power of cumulative efforts. Thus, if we view a snapshot of each day along the way, no single day's accomplishments would look extraordinary or monumental. However, by making these efforts day after day, the individual created a

momentum that propelled him or her to the desired destination. Remember, you don't climb a mountain with one giant leap.

7. **There are no guarantees.** By the way, is there a chance that you could embark on a challenging goal ... and *not* reach it? Absolutely. But, when you set an ambitious objective and give it your all, you are a winner and can hold your head high regardless of the end result.

So, do you think that you could double or triple your income — or come up with an idea that could be worth thousands, or even millions, of dollars to your company? Or is there something that you'd like to accomplish in your community, but you've been wondering what you, as one person, could do to make a difference? Whatever your big dream might be, don't worry that it is "unrealistic." People are achieving "unrealistic" goals every day. As Thomas Edison said: "If we all did the things we are capable of doing, we would literally astound ourselves."

26

What's Inside Your Bubble?

I will not let anyone
walk through my mind with their dirty feet.

— Mahatma Gandhi

Have you ever seen the television movie, "*The Boy in the Plastic Bubble*?" Released in 1976 and starring John Travolta, the movie was based on the true story of a teenage boy whose immune system did not function. As a result, he was vulnerable to the most common germs that all of us come in contact with every day. Since the boy could die from exposure to germs, he had to live inside a plastic bubble, which served as a sterile environment to protect him.

There's a connection here to our lives. In a way, we all live inside a "bubble," an environment we create, consisting of the influences we allow into our lives. These influences include the people we interact with, the materials we read, the things we watch on TV and so on. We can allow positive influences into our bubble, negative influences, or a mixture of the two.

The influences that you allow into your environment have access to something very precious — your mind! What you invite into your mind affects what you think about and how you feel. This, in turn, shapes your attitude, your beliefs and your behaviors … and ultimately your results.

Now and again, it's a good idea to re-evaluate what you've allowed into your bubble. Here are some suggestions for making your bubble more positive so you can lead a happier, more productive life:

- **Limit your exposure to the television news**. We're now being bombarded with negativity on the so-called news reports. I call it "Media Madness." Terror attacks, crimes, and other tragedies dominate. You rarely hear any uplifting stories. Instead, the news anchors focus on violence and destruction, and you often get graphic pictures to cement the horror even further in your brain. But why stop there? Most news reports now have a "runner" that goes along the bottom of the screen so you can get additional negative news in print while you're hearing about the other catastrophes. If you continue to view these programs for hours on end, you're allowing an avalanche of gloom into your mind. You can keep up with current events by watching the news for about 10 minutes. Don't let this poisonous material into your bubble for too long or the negativity will take its toll on your success and well-being.

- **Maintain relationships that are uplifting**. I'm referring here to your discretionary relationships, where you have a choice whether to spend time with the other person. This includes your friends and also people you spend time with at work. For instance, you might have a habit of hanging around with negative people at lunch, listening to them complain about this or that, or even engaging in "water cooler gossip" yourself. This is your choice, and you could choose to be with more positive people or to simply eat lunch alone. When you invite negative people into your bubble, they will constantly pour their negative comments into your mind. This helps to kill your attitude and your dreams.

Think about it—how do you feel when you're around these prophets of doom? You're drained because these people take energy from you. Positive, supportive people, on the other hand, provide an infusion of energy and help to boost your attitude. Consider the people in your bubble and whether you need to make some adjustments.

♦ **Program your mind with positive materials.** If I were to say that your attitude and your beliefs are dictating the course of your life, many of you would nod your head in agreement. But let me ask you this: How much time did you spend today monitoring your attitude? How much time did you spend today concentrating on your beliefs? How much time did you spend today considering your enormous potential? Chances are you didn't spend *any* time thinking about these vital subjects.

Whether or not you care to admit it, you're programming your mind every day. It's just a matter of whether you choose positive programming or negative programming. Positive programming improves your attitude and encourages you to take constructive action. Negative inputs weaken your attitude and discourage you from moving forward. To improve the quality of your bubble, make sure to get positive messages into your mind every day. Spend 15-30 minutes each morning reading something positive, whether from a book, a magazine or online. Spend 15-30 minutes listening to positive audio programs every day. In the very first week, you're going to see results in the way you think and act. Your bubble is going to be a lot more positive and supportive than ever before.

♦ **Set the mood with music.** What's your favorite song? Maybe you have a few songs that bring up positive memories, make you smile or give you a burst of energy.

If I played your favorite songs for you right now, you'd instantly feel better. As I see it, people don't use music often enough to create a positive mood. Whether in your car, at home, or while exercising, play music that will help you create the mood you want. If you want energy, play music that invigorates you (the theme from the movie, "Rocky," might be one example). If you want to relax after a stressful day, play music that calms you or helps you think about peaceful, serene experiences in your life. Make sure that your bubble is filled with music that works for you.

Just as the teenage "boy in the bubble" took control of his environment, you too have this ability. Make the commitment to carefully examine every influence that you invite into your environment. Your success and your happiness depend on the choices you make.

27

Success Is Child's Play!

You're never too old to become younger.

— Mae West

We can learn a great deal about the qualities and behaviors that lead to success and fulfillment in life simply by observing children. I myself attended a mini-success seminar just the other day while sitting in a local sandwich shop.

There I was, eating my turkey sandwich, when a mother entered the store with her two young kids—a boy and a girl who each looked to be about four or five years old. The mother had her hands full of clothing she had just picked up from the dry cleaners. The frown and harried look on her face said that she just wanted to get out of the store quickly and go home.

While mom waited on line for her order to be taken, the two children ran over to the self-serve soda machine and ice dispenser to check out all the gadgets. It was a typical contraption—the kind where you just tap the button and an avalanche of ice plops into your cup (and, probably, onto the floor!).

The young boy was sticking his hands through the grill where the excess soda and ice falls in. He was trying to feel and get a handful of whatever sticky stuff was down there. His mother caught a glimpse and shouted at him to get his hands out of there. Oblivious to her command, the boy kept putting his hands through the grill, investigating the mess.

The young girl then started pointing to each item on the machine and yelled over to her mother, "What's that?" — eager to hear mom's explanation of each flavor. Mom, however, wasn't interested in playing teacher. She paid for the drink, received an empty cup, and attempted to fill it herself. Her kids, of course, had other ideas.

Both children wanted to operate the machine. They begged Mom to allow them to do it, refusing to take NO for an answer — and believe me, mom did say NO several times before finally relenting. Both youngsters excitedly grabbed the cup and pressed it against the ice and soda levers. The cup was wobbly and not centered properly, but they didn't care. They just wanted to be involved and to have fun.

Here's what I learned from these children:

1. **The children were totally engaged in the present moment.** How difficult it is for us as adults to concentrate on NOW and to block out all other thoughts. Either we're brooding over the past or worrying about the future, seldom taking the time to experience and enjoy the fullness of the present. Not so for these kids. Nothing in the world mattered except that soda dispenser. They weren't dwelling on what went wrong yesterday and they certainly weren't concerned about their college education or even what was for dinner that night. They were completely absorbed by what they were doing at that moment.

2. **The youngsters had a goal which excited them.** They knew what they wanted, which was to operate the machine and drink the soda. All of their energies were directed toward the achievement of that goal. How many adults have clearly defined goals that excite them? Sadly, the "goal" for many is just to get through the day. It doesn't have to be this way, though.

You don't need to fall into a rut and put your life on "auto pilot." Instead, you have the ability to choose a challenging, exciting goal to which you can strive.

3. **The kids were incredibly persistent.** They were going to operate the machine no matter what mom said! Every time they heard "NO," they kept on insisting until their mother finally gave in. They had their eyes on the goal and no obstacle would get in their way.

The determination of these children reminded me of the statistics generated from studies of salespeople. Many sales are closed after the prospect has said "NO" five or six times, yet few salespeople are willing to persist and ask for the sale after one or two "NO"s. Now, I'm not suggesting that you keep begging and refuse to leave your prospect's office until he or she places an order. But we should learn to be persistent and to search for creative new ways to turn a "NO" into a "YES" — whether we're on a sales call, negotiating with our employer or launching a new project in our community.

4. **The kids were filled with wonder and enthusiasm.** Once they saw the machine, they wanted to know everything about it. They were excited and bubbling with enthusiasm at the thought of selecting a flavor and filling the cup.

Contrast this approach with the way adults tend to view new things. Most of us are rarely enthused about the unknown. In fact, we usually keep our distance and have no interest in exploring anything unfamiliar. Furthermore, as we resign ourselves to staying entirely within our "comfort zone," we begin to close our minds not only to new ideas that may cross our path, but to the miracles and wonders which always surround us. For instance, many of us take for granted the rotation of the planets, the movement of the ocean or the extraordinary transformation of a caterpillar into a butterfly. Let's wake up!

5. The children didn't care what others thought about them. Even though I was just a short distance away and staring right at them, these children paid no attention to me. They weren't concerned about how well they were "performing." In fact, failure wasn't on their minds at all. The cup was tilted and ice and soda were all over the place ... yet they couldn't care less! They just wanted to learn, participate and enjoy themselves.

As we get older, we begin to focus not so much on doing a task, but rather on the possibility that others may laugh at us or judge our performance harshly. As a result, we often decide that it's best not to try at all. If this has happened to you, it's time to get back in the game. Give it your best and participate. (You see, the truth is, nobody cares that much about you anyway; most people are too busy worrying about their own problems!)

So, let's make it a point to recapture some of our "child's play" of years past. Think about the ways in which you can apply these ideas to your life. For example, do you have a goal which excites you? If not, maybe it's time to set one that will rekindle your enthusiasm. Or, are you holding back from pursuing something because you are concerned about how others will judge you? Here's your chance to get involved and stop looking over your shoulder. If nothing else, make it a point to start observing *and learning from* children.

I'm not suggesting that you discard the valuable traits you have developed as an adult and revert solely to "childish" behavior. The key is to integrate both approaches. When we combine adult maturity and discipline with the playfulness, inquisitiveness and creativity of the child within us, we can accomplish great things — and have plenty of fun and enjoyment along the way.

28

It's More Than
One Person's Opinion

Facts do not cease to exist because they are ignored.
— Aldous Huxley

A co-worker comes to you and mentions that you look a little tired. You're a bit surprised by the comment and start to think, "It's true that I haven't gotten much sleep lately, but I didn't think it was noticeable. Oh, well, it's only one person's opinion."

Think again. The reality is, there are probably several others in your office who have noticed the very same thing. They simply haven't said anything to you. The same holds true for other aspects of your appearance, whether it's your hairstyle or the clothes you wear. When one person voices an opinion, chances are that others hold the same view. Often, the comments are flattering, such as "that is a very attractive suit" or "your shirt color complements your complexion." Here again, even if the remarks come from only one person, others are thinking likewise.

This principle also applies to your business dealings. When one customer raises a problem with some aspect of your product or service—e.g., that the receptionist or desk clerk was rude—it's quite likely that other customers have the same opinion. And, when you hear the same complaint or compliment from four of five people, rest assured that a **multiple** of that number concur with this evaluation.

Finally, let's consider how this concept applies to your human relations skills. If someone tells you that you're continually interrupting, maybe it's time to take a look at how often you do, in fact, interrupt people before they have completed what they want to say. And, how about your attitude? Has anybody complimented you on your optimistic outlook, or have you heard once or twice that you complain too often ... or that you rarely smile?

It comes down to this: frequently, we get comfortable in our established patterns and grow blind to certain personal or business habits that we possess. We simply don't see what is **obvious** to others.

Now, I'm not trying to get you to be overly self-conscious, to be a conformist or to change simply to please others. But, let's face it. The vast majority of life takes place while we are relating to other people, whether face-to-face, on the phone, in a letter or on the internet. Most anything that we want to accomplish — from getting a promotion to getting a haircut — involves interacting with those around us. So, it's vital to be aware of the way others perceive us [and to make changes where appropriate] if we hope to move forward in the direction of our goals.

Here are guidelines to assist you in getting a "reality check" from time to time so that you can be more effective in your business and personal affairs:

1. **Keep your antennae up.** When someone makes a comment to you, even if it's in the form of a joke (remember: people often mask criticism with humor), pay attention. *Ask yourself:* Have I heard a similar remark before? Let the comments sink in.

2. **Solicit feedback.** This isn't easy for most people, as we tend to avoid looking too closely at ourselves.

Nevertheless, do it. Keep in mind not to ask for *negative* feedback only. It's equally important to reinforce your positive characteristics.

Who can provide this needed input? Well, if you work for an organization, it goes without saying that your managers, colleagues and customers may have a thing or two to contribute. And, if you're a business owner, it's vital to maintain open lines of communication with both employees and customers. On issues such as appearance or personal traits, ask a spouse, friend or co-worker for their thoughts.

3. **Don't be defensive.** It's useless to encourage feedback if you're going to justify your current behaviors. You're not trying to win an argument, or to change the other person's mind. Simply listen to what's being said.

As you've read this article, I'll bet that a few issues have already crossed your mind ... questions that you have about your business, your appearance, your personal traits or interpersonal skills. Make a written list of these items right now and begin to invite comments from others.

It bears repeating: Don't make changes just for the sake of pleasing others. Maintain your uniqueness, and if you're happy with a particular behavior — and it's not hurting anyone else — stick with it. However, that doesn't mean you should put your head in the sand and ignore the effect of your present conduct.

It takes courage to look within and to ask others to offer their views. Yet, you won't grow and improve unless you continually examine yourself and your business or career. The adjustments you make can have a profound impact on your ultimate happiness and success in life.

29

Negative Thinking
Never Helps

*There is no law by which one can
as long as he thinks he can't.*

— Orison Swett Marden

I've never had someone come up to me and say, "I'm always negative and it's working out great for me. I can't wait to get up in the morning!" And yet, positive thinking still has its skeptics. Some people tell me that positive thinking doesn't work or that it's "unrealistic," especially in today's turbulent world.

"Look around you," they say. "How can you be so positive?" Well, let me ask you this: can the world be lifted out of negativity by adding MORE negativity?

The truth is, there are certain things that negative thinking will do for you. It will make you sick. It will make you very unpleasant to be around. And, it will significantly limit what you can achieve.

Let's take a closer look at why negative thinking doesn't serve us. For starters, we all operate under the Law of Dominant Thought. Simply stated, we're always moving in the direction of our dominant thoughts. Most of us have heard about the "self-fulfilling prophecy"—that we get what we expect in life. Expect negative results and, sure enough, you'll produce negative results.

As I'm sure you've found, negative thinking also causes you to feel more stress and to have less energy. How many times have you gotten sick during a stressful period in your life?

If you're still not convinced about the effects of being negative, take out a sheet of paper and write down your list of all the benefits you're getting from negative thinking. I think your list is going to be very short, if you come up with anything at all.

Let me make an important distinction here. It's quite natural for a person to feel sad in response to a tragedy or the death of a loved one. There's a period of loss and grieving that differs for each individual, and we don't expect a grief stricken person to be positive in the short run. However, even a person in that situation will not be served by holding onto their negative thoughts indefinitely. (By the way, if you've suffered some trauma or have had a difficult time releasing negative thinking, by all means get counseling. That's not a sign of weakness. It's a constructive step to help you move forward in your life.)

Doing What Comes Naturally

From everything I've observed, babies are naturally positive. They're usually smiling and seem to be enjoying life. I haven't met any negative, frowning babies. That's why I don't buy the argument that negative thinking is just natural. Those who think negatively do so out of habit. They have conditioned themselves to think that way.

In Western societies in particular, we've developed the tendency to focus on minor irritations, even though these annoyances are only a tiny part of our overall lives. We tend to focus on the 5% of our lives that are going "wrong" ... instead of the 95% going well. We'll sigh and tell everyone about the traffic jam or flat tire on the way to work. Yet, we'll never comment about the miracle of our existence—the billions of cells in our body that somehow allow our brain to function, our heart to pump blood or our eyes to see. We don't appreciate that we have enough food to eat or that we have a roof over our heads, while there are millions of people who don't have these gifts.

It's no wonder that so many people think negatively. The newspaper is filled with negative news. Television and radio reports dwell on tragedies and crimes. How often do you read or hear about people helping each other or doing something positive? Hardly ever. If you do nothing to counteract this bombardment of negativity, you're going to think negatively.

At any time, however, you could take control of this situation. You could stop watching and listening to all of the negative news and read something positive instead. You could limit your contact with "toxic" people and make sure your life is filled with positive inputs. If you did that, your "natural" inclination would switch and you'd begin to think positively.

Quick Mental Exercises

I'll show you that you have much more control over your thinking than you might believe. Try this experiment. Right now, think about your favorite movie. You might even get a picture in your mind of your favorite scene in that movie. Now, let's think about your favorite meal. What is it? A fresh salad … a juicy steak … grilled salmon? Whatever it is, just think about it. Now that your mouth is watering, let's move on. Think about being out in a snowstorm, with two feet of snow on the ground. Can you see the snow and feel the cold on your toes?

In each case, you were able to control what you thought about. You could shift your thinking in an instant.

It has been said that positive thinking is harmful because optimistic people ignore things that can go wrong or are easily duped and taken advantage of. In other words, if you expect the sun to be shining all the time, you're just naïve and are sure to be disappointed. But positive thinking doesn't mean that you ignore reality or refuse to consider the obstacles that might arise. On the contrary, the positive person expects a positive outcome but prepares for overcoming obstacles.

For example, if a positive person is planning an outdoor wedding, he or she won't use the power of positive thinking to make sure it doesn't rain on the big day. Rather, a positive person is prepared with contingency plans, focusing on things that she can directly control, such as having a tent available in case it does rain.

By this point, I hope that you're receptive to the idea that negative thinking won't help us. So, the question is: how can we change our thinking to become more positive? The answer, simply stated, is that you must change what goes into your mind every day. Start by eliminating as many of the negative inputs as possible. While you can listen to the news for a few minutes to catch the important headlines, there is no need to hear reports of the same murders and bombings over and over each day. At the same time, replace the negative inputs with positive stimuli. Read positive materials on a daily basis. Listen to positive audio programs, or to music that inspires or relaxes you.

Here's another technique: monitor your everyday language. When you find yourself beginning to complain or talk negatively, switch immediately to something positive. Say something like, "I really have so much to be grateful for" and start listing some of those things. Condition yourself to focus on constructive solutions to challenges, rather than harping on problems or fretting about things outside of your control.

Make a commitment for the next 30 days. Think about what you want instead of what you don't want. Think about what you're grateful for rather than what you believe is missing in your life. Saturate your mind with the positive. After 30 days, you can then decide whether to keep focusing on the positive or to revert to your negative thinking pattern. I think I know which one you'll choose!

30

Live in the Past ... and
It Will Become Your Future

Never let yesterday use up today.
— Richard H. Nelson

I enjoy speaking with people who come up to me after one of my presentations to let me know a little about their background and experiences. Sometimes, however, these people will introduce themselves — and in less than a minute, they're telling me about some negative experience that has held them back in life. It goes something like this: "My name is John, and my father was an alcoholic," or "My name is Marilyn, and I grew up in this really dysfunctional family."

Before you send me a letter asking me to be more sensitive to people with past hurts, hear me out. I'm not saying that people with past trauma or negative feelings should deny that those events happened or refuse to acknowledge their feelings. In fact, I would encourage these people to seek counseling from mental health professionals or to visit a doctor if they have physical ailments. Everyone falls into the trap of discussing unpleasant circumstances, and I'm no exception. Yet, I think it's important in these instances to ask ourselves: *"How long will I **choose** to dwell on this* *negative experience? Why do I inject this topic into **all** of my conversations? Is this helping to create better results in my life?"*

I think we'd all agree that Oprah Winfrey is a positive role model who has accomplished some extraordinary things in her life. As you probably know, Oprah was sexually molested and abused as a young girl. She never denies this aspect of her past and readily admits that it still affects her. Yet she doesn't begin every one of her shows by saying, "Hi, this is Oprah and I was abused as a child." If she did that, she would never have reached the place where she is now. I'll bet that the majority of her attention is on the things she can do today and in the future to make a positive difference in the world. Simply put, she doesn't dwell on the abuse she suffered years ago. That's a choice she has made, and we can all learn from her.

Author and speaker Eckhart Tolle talks about the way we live in the past and keep telling people our "story." We tell it to everyone we come across. And generally the story is heavily concentrated on negative events rather than on positive, uplifting experiences. We tend to drag our story around like a ball and chain attached to our ankles, pointing to it and anxious to provide all the gory details.

Where does that get us? Well, it might elicit some sympathy. Along those lines, it might also get us involved in some very time-consuming negative conversations with other "story-tellers" who are all too eager to try to "top" our tale of woe with one of their own. ("If you think that's bad, well, let me tell you about ... .") And perhaps our story is something we use as an excuse for why we're not out there living up to our fullest potential. You see, if we have this horrible handicap, there's no use trying to achieve anything great. We can continue to live in our comfort zone of limitation.

By the way, this isn't confined to stories involving severe trauma. For instance, some people tell you about how they were unfairly fired from a job six months ago or how their allergies are acting up. They may tell you that they are not appreciated at work.

Whether you're thinking and talking about a tragic event or even a minor irritation, you're working against yourself and just perpetuating negative conditions. There is a Law of Dominant Thought, which states that we're always moving in the direction of our currently dominant thoughts. That's why it's so important to keep your focus on what you want instead of what you don't want. Said another way, *what you focus on expands.*

We don't achieve our objectives in life by contemplating (or discussing) the opposite of what we want to attain. We don't attract wealth when we contemplate being broke. We don't get healthy by contemplating how sick we are ... and how bad we feel.

Even if you talk about the event while mentioning a desire to change it, you're still reinforcing the negative event. For instance, you might keep saying to yourself and others, "I keep eating too much ice cream day after day and I need to stop doing that." Your mind hears "ice cream" and will want more ice cream! It's far better to think about having a healthy body and to start eating more fruits and vegetables.

Here's an important qualification: you're going to find that when you **do** have a painful experience, whether it's an illness, the death of a loved one or even losing your job, the wound is raw and you'll find yourself talking about the incident often. In fact, many people will ask you about it. Thus, talking about it is only natural. Your mission is to put the event behind you as quickly as possible. In other words, stop thinking and talking about the past event as soon as you can. No one can tell you what length of time is appropriate. It depends on your unique situation. Remember, this isn't about denial. It's about moving your life forward in a positive direction.

Today, and in the future, notice when you find yourself thinking and talking about negative conditions or negative experiences of your past ... unless, of course, you *want* to reinforce your pain and suffering and create more of it in the days to come. Now's the time to let go of the past, so you can tell a new, happier story in the future.

31

Every Day Is Thanksgiving!

Gratitude helps you grow and expand;
gratitude brings joy and laughter into your life
and into the lives of all those around you.

— Eileen Caddy

Did anything *great* happen to you in the last 24 hours? I mean something monumental ... something you're so thankful for that you felt like breaking out in song? Go ahead, review your day.

Maybe you're thinking about whether you received any checks in the mail; or, perhaps, you're just delighted because today's mail didn't include any bills! As you consider this question, you might reach the conclusion that nothing truly spectacular occurred.

But, hold on for a moment.

Did you have a place to stay last night, shielded from the elements? Imagine what it might be like if you and your family didn't have a roof over your heads.

Is there a bathroom, plumbing or hot water where you live? Does that make your life a little more comfortable?

From the time you awoke, did you have the use of your eyesight to see the sun and the beautiful blue sky? Were you able to get out of bed, walk around and go outside? Some people won't have that luxury today.

How about your hearing? Can you hear the sounds of the birds chirping or the wind rustling through the trees? At breakfast, could you smell the fresh coffee brewing or the toast after it popped up in the toaster? What would a day be like if you couldn't hear or smell ... or if you couldn't taste your food? Yes, there ARE people who don't have the full use of these senses.

And what about those things that aren't necessary to survive, but that enhance your day-to-day existence — items like a car, a radio, a television or a computer? Are you truly thankful for these and other gifts you regularly use?

Celebrate Each Precious Gift

I'm sure that you get my point. Each day, we have dozens of reasons to give thanks. Yet, we generally take these things for granted and fail to see them as precious items to be cherished. Of course, when any *one* of them is taken from us, even temporarily, we take notice. But, day in and day out, we rarely consider our blessings.

Why am I making such a big fuss about this? It's simple. When you focus on gratitude and other positive emotions, you feel better and are more relaxed, more creative and more productive. You also have a positive influence on those around you, at work and at home.

Here, then, are a few things you can do to cultivate an "attitude of gratitude" in your life:

1. **Think about your blessings daily.** The key is to develop a habit of focusing on things you are grateful for. Put a note on your bathroom mirror or carry a card in your wallet or purse with the message, "Count Your Blessings." Set aside time each day to reflect on how fortunate you are. This isn't a time-consuming chore, and you'll be amazed at the results!

2. **Verbalize your gratitude.** During conversations at work and at home, express your appreciation for all

of the wonderful things and people in your life. If you live in a country that allows you freedom of expression and the right to pursue your dreams, tell others how much you appreciate that. Express your gratitude to supportive coworkers and family members. Call your parents and let them know how much you value the sacrifices they made for you while you were growing up.

3. **Shift the focus away from difficulties.** When problems arise and you've done all you can to remedy them, train your mind to bring your attention back to your blessings. This helps you to keep things in perspective — e.g., recognizing that your health and basic necessities in life are more important than the fact that the office copier will be out of order for a few hours. Besides, when you are relaxed and experiencing positive emotions, you stand a far better chance of coming up with solutions to your difficulties.

4. **Lift others in need.** One of the best ways to use your gifts (health, energy, attitude, etc.) is to share them with others who are having a rough time. Can you lend a helping hand to a coworker, friend, relative or other person in your community? Merely spending time with someone in need, or giving a few words of encouragement can make a tremendous difference to that person, while helping you to develop a deeper sense of gratitude about how well-off you are.

It costs you nothing to be grateful and appreciative, yet it has a considerable impact on the quality of your life. So, don't waste another minute. Every day, reflect on the priceless gifts you've been enjoying. Openly share your gratitude with others.

And, the next time somebody asks if anything great happened to you today, you'll have plenty to say!

32

What Does Success Mean to You?

*Success based on anything but internal
fulfillment is bound to be empty.*

— Dr. Martha Friedman

You've been invited by a college in your area to deliver the commencement address at graduation ceremonies. More specifically, the President of the college wants you to speak to the graduates about your definition of "success" and what constitutes a "successful life." Not such a simple assignment, is it?

Sure, lots of people talk about success. It's a word we use all the time. And, in fact, if you were to ask people to define success, you'd probably hear the following responses:

- Success is about making money.
- Success is about having material possessions.
- Success is about career achievements.
- Success is about having loving family relationships.
- Success is about raising well-adjusted children.
- Success is about spiritual growth.
- Success is about making a difference in the world.

Of course, many would say that success is a combination of these items. What about you? Are you ready to give that commencement address right now ... or do you need some time to think about your personal definition of "success" and a "successful life."

As you ponder your own definition of success, here are some questions to consider:

1. **Is this really MY definition, or is it someone else's?** We're being programmed constantly as to what "success" *should* mean to us. If you watch TV, you see all the celebrities being glorified. Their every move is covered. If you had just dropped in from another planet and turned on the TV, you'd think that success was measured by notoriety, fame and fortune. You watch commercials that show how you should want to look. Who ever came up with the idea of creating "six-pack" abdominal muscles? And the worst thing is not to have a full head of hair. You can't have thinning hair and be successful, can you? And, of course, the car you drive says a lot about you as well. The subliminal message is that if you look a certain way and have certain possessions, you're successful. Growing up, your parents or relatives may have exerted influence to steer you in a direction they thought would make you a "success." Dig deep to find out what you truly feel constitutes a successful life. The graduates don't need to hear what others think about success — they need to hear what YOU think!

2. **Has my definition of success changed over the years?** If you're learning and growing as a person, your concept of what success means to you will constantly change and evolve. Early in life, you may think that success is primarily about getting a good job or earning a good living. As the years pass, your focus may shift to the meaningfulness of your work or to

your family relationships. There's an excellent chance that you'll place more emphasis on spiritual growth as the years pass. I don't think there ever comes a point where our definition of success is "set in stone." That definition keeps changing as we mature. You just might want to share with the graduates the evolution of your views on success, so they'll know what to expect.

3. **Are my activities consistent with my definition?** In my experience, the overwhelming majority of people do not live in a way that is consistent with their stated definition of success. You may say that success means a rewarding family life. However, if you're working all the time and spend little time with your family, then your behavior reveals your "true" priority. The challenge is to determine what your "real" definition of success is ... and then make the commitment to act in accordance with that definition. What tips can you give the graduates to help them in this area?

I'm guessing that the ideas are flowing for you now. You've probably thought about many other issues that I haven't raised on this subject of success. Take some time now to write down notes as to what you're going to say in your commencement address. Who knows? You just may be asked to give that speech one day. And even if you don't, this is an exercise that can open your eyes and change your life.

33

A Shoe Shine to Remember

*Every adversity carries with it the seed
of an equal or greater benefit.*

— Napoleon Hill

I like to think of myself as an industrious person with a lot of discipline. But there's one thing I just can't bring myself to do. It seems so simple and yet I will not do it. You see, *I hate shining my shoes.* So, when I want my shoes shined, I take them somewhere to get it done. It's simple enough if I'm in New York City where there are plenty of stands to get your shoes shined for a few dollars.

When I'm home on Long Island, though, it's a little more difficult. Here's what I've been doing for years. I drive to a shopping mall that's around 12 miles from my home. There's a store in the mall that has a shoe shine stand. While I'm at the store, I buy a few things that I need and get my shoes shined. Usually, I bring in a few pair of shoes at a time.

Well, I was about to go out of town for several days and needed to have some shoes shined. The shoe shine stand in the store opens at 10:30 am, so I arrived at 10:40. The stand was still closed. So, I went to buy some belts and a shirt in the same store. I came back to the stand at 11:00 — still closed. I asked one of the store employees, "Is the shoe shine stand open today?"

"Yes," he replied. "The person who shines the shoes is here, and he'll be coming out in a minute to open the stand." So, I waited … for about 10 minutes. No one showed up. So, I asked another employee nearby. He told me the stand would be open in just a minute. So, I waited another ten minutes. No one showed up. I walked up to the counter and spoke to someone who said he was the manager of this department. I told him what had happened and that I had waited 20 minutes for the stand to open.

He told me, "The person who does the shoe shines hasn't shown up today. I'm sorry some other people told you he was here." The manager was busy and went back to another customer. I had "the look" — you know, the look you get when you feel you've been treated unfairly and your business is not appreciated.

My thoughts immediately went to: "I've waited here for more than 20 minutes and I'm not going to stand for this kind of treatment." Who can I report this to?" My mind was running wild. *I'll register my complaint with the store … then I'll follow up with a letter … and, if that doesn't work, I could petition the Supreme Court!* My blood pressure was rising and I was really focused on the negative. Then 20 years of mental training by reading and listening to motivational materials kicked in.

I called an immediate "time out" and calmed down. Was it really worth ruining my day and spending the next 48 hours figuring out ways to register my dissatisfaction with the way I was treated at a shoe shine stand? No way. After all, what's the *best* that could happen? The store would say "I'm sorry" and maybe they'd give me a $10 gift certificate. Was it worth ruining two days of my life? So, I came to my senses and quietly left the store, without reporting the incident to anyone.

As I drove home, I just let it go. I was feeling better already. But, as I was getting off the parkway near my home, a thought popped into my head: "Stop at the shoe store near the exit." This is a store where I go to buy shoes on occasion. Then, logic took over and I said to myself, "Why on earth would I go to that shoe store now? How are they going to help me get my shoes shined?" But, since it was only a few blocks out of my way, I drove to that store.

I saw a salesman I knew there and told him I was having trouble finding someone who could shine a particular pair of leather shoes I had bought there. I asked if he had any suggestions. He told me that just up the road there was a shoe repair shop where the owner could help me. So, I drove to the shop. The door to the store was locked. There was a sign that said "Be back in five minutes." Another obstacle. Should I leave or wait? I was really tempted to leave, but I decided to stay put.

About ten minutes later, the owner returned. I told him I needed to get some shoes shined right away. He told me to leave the shoes with him and to come back in one hour. All the shoes would be shined, he said. I came back in an hour and not only were the shoes shined, they were glistening! The cost of the shine was the same as the shine I'd been getting at the store in the mall, but this shine was about five times better.

The bottom line: I found a new place to get my shoes shined ... at the same price ... with far better quality ... and much closer to my home.

This shoe shine incident illustrates so many important motivational principles:

Get out of the revenge mode immediately. Revenge and persistent complaining wastes your time and drains your energy. As your thoughts race with the steps you'll take to register your dissatisfaction, call a "time out" and get quiet. Recognize the price you're going to pay for pursuing your complaint and consider whether it's worth ruining your attitude for hours and sacrificing a day or two of productivity. (Of course, there are some instances where it is appropriate to register a genuine complaint and seek some sort of compensation. However, in most cases, pursuing a trivial issue because you feel "wronged" is absolutely not worth the effort.)

Trust your intuition. That voice in our head can tell us some pretty strange things. Yet, the more illogical it is, the more I've learned to pay attention to it (this assumes the advice is legal and moral). There was no logical reason for me to stop at that shoe store on my drive home. But I followed that "advice" and it led me to discover the new shoe repair shop. Life gives messages in its own way, and it's not always the way you expected.

Persist through the obstacles. Even when you're focusing on the positive and trusting your instincts, there will be bumps along the road. I had been to the mall, then to the shoe store and then to the shoe repair shop. My final "test" was to find the repair shop closed. I was tempted to leave at that point and say "It wasn't meant to be." But I persisted and waited another 10 minutes, and it was sure worth it! Remember that even when you're headed in the right direction, you'll be faced with disappointments and obstacles. Don't give up if you want to get to the good stuff!

Every adversity has a positive side. At the time I left the shopping mall, all I thought was that I had wasted a lot of time and still hadn't gotten my shoes shined. However, if you interviewed me two hours later, I would have told you that I was delighted that the shopping mall incident happened because it led me to discover a much better shoe shine closer to my home and with far better quality. Being "stood up" at the shoe shine stand in the mall turned out to be a blessing. But I never would have received this blessing had I not abandoned my immediate negative thoughts and allowed a more positive outcome to unfold.

Little things have big consequences. The employees and the manager at the store in the mall didn't give any thought to the fact that I was given the wrong information and waited 20 minutes at their shoe shine stand. To them, it was a little thing. *Wrong!* Now that I've found a better shoe shine closer to home (at the same price), I won't have to go to that store anymore for shoe shines. And that also means I won't be buying many belts, shirts and other items at that store. They lost a considerable amount of business by not appreciating my time.

Obviously, this isn't about my shoes. It's about **your life**. The lessons here apply to all of us, day after day. You may experience something today or tomorrow that will involve these principles. So, the next time, you're about to let an adverse circumstance lead you down a negative path, take a deep breath, think about my glistening shoes, and open your mind to the silver lining that's just waiting to be discovered.

34

Surrender Your Ego

If you are all wrapped up in yourself,
you are overdressed.

— Kate Halverson

You hear someone bragging about his accomplishments and you think to yourself, "Boy, that guy has quite an ego." Or, someone at work won't stop arguing until you admit that she's right and you're wrong. In both cases, you're turned off by this ego-driven behavior, and you feel distant from such people.

When I say *ego*, I'm not referring to classic psychiatric and psychological definitions used by Freud. I'm talking about the feelings of self-importance and separation—where we attempt, consciously or unconsciously, to establish our superiority over others.

The ego feels a sense of incompleteness and seeks external input to fill the void. Eckhart Tolle, in his excellent book, *The Power of Now*, puts it this way: "The most common ego identifications have to do with possessions: the work you do, social status and recognition, knowledge and education, physical appearance ... and also political, nationalistic, racial, religious and other collective identifications. None of these is *you*."

By this, he means that none of these items is your identity … who you truly are. Rather, they represent temporary possessions or labels that you accumulate.

How can you tell when your ego is exerting influence and interfering with your relationships and the quality of your life? Here are some of the classic signs.

You're concerned about titles. The ego is always worried about your place in the hierarchy. Do you care about your title at work and whether you could get a promotion with an even more significant title? Many people are willing to forego a raise or other benefits as long as they can get a more prestigious title next to their name. When you really get down to it, titles are meaningless and tend to enhance separation in any organization. In this respect, I think we can learn a lot from the Quakers, who don't use titles because it goes against the principle that all people are equal.

You're constantly comparing yourself with others. The ego sees you "in competition" with everyone else on the planet. You think that somehow you'll feel better if you "score" higher than people in certain categories. You want to look better than others and be smarter than them. You compare your income and material possessions with those of your neighbors and co-workers. This is a fruitless game that will never bring you satisfaction no matter how much you accumulate or how fabulous you look.

You find yourself arguing that you're right and others are wrong. I'm sure you can identify with this one! You're having a discussion with your spouse or friend and you're adamant that you're right — and that the other person is wrong. If he or she won't admit it, you keep piling up evidence to support your claim. Naturally, the other party seldom admits to being "wrong," no matter how strong your argument. (In fact, there is likely no clear right or wrong to begin with.)

In the end, the other person resents your stubbornness and insistence to be right. You've lost even if you "won" the argument. This strategy destroys relationships, with no corresponding benefit other than stroking your ego. You don't have to agree with the other person's position. You can learn to state your position without declaring a winner and loser.

You frequently judge or criticize others. I'll be the first to admit that suspending judgment or withholding criticism is often quite a challenge. We've been conditioned to criticize and judge others. Now, there *is* such a thing as constructive criticism, and we should strive to help others to improve. However, we often criticize to demonstrate that we know more ... or that we're superior to others. This is destructive criticism that comes from the ego. We think that by putting down others, we can elevate ourselves. It may feel this way, but in reality, all we're doing is covering up for our own lack of self-esteem.

You're extremely self-conscious about your appearance. It's great to be clean and well-groomed. That's not what I'm talking about here. I'm referring to those who are fixated on every ounce of body fat even if they're slim. These are the people who try to look 20 years of age forever and run for facelifts and other cosmetic fads. What on earth is wrong with a wrinkle or two? I used to be self-conscious about losing some hair on the top of my head. I then came to grips with the fact that it's not a big deal but a natural part of life. Your ego tells you that people won't love you or respect you unless you look "young." What nonsense! I cringe (there I go "judging") when I see all the celebrities with their faces pulled tight by plastic surgeries and their lips swollen by injections. I don't find that attractive in the slightest. Do you? By the way, I think it's great to exercise, lift weights and tone your muscles— not to impress other people, but because it makes you healthier, increases your stamina and you feel better about yourself.

You live almost exclusively in the past or the future. The ego wants you to re-live the past (especially the negative stuff!) and to worry about the future. So, you beat yourself up for the things you did months or years ago, even though there's nothing you can do about it now. Or, you worry about how things in the future will unfold and how you can protect yourself.

Now that you're aware of some of the signs that the ego is "acting up," what can you do to break some of the ego's power over you? You've already taken the first step, which is awareness. By simply shining the spotlight on some of the ego's favorite tricks (and reviewing this list often) you'll begin to diminish these destructive activities and thought patterns. When you find yourself comparing yourself with others, you'll say to yourself, "There I go comparing myself..." and you'll do less comparing in the future.

The other way to tame the ego is to live in the present moment as much as possible. The ego hates the present moment because that's where you lose your feelings of separation and feel connected to everything in the universe. Spend at least 10-15 minutes every day in solitude. Just close your eyes and think about nothing, other than focusing on your breathing. You'll see that this is not an easy thing to do! Your mind is filled with chatter and won't want to calm down. Just let the thoughts drift away and after a minute or two, you'll feel a sense of peace.

The martial arts and disciplines such as yoga and tai chi also train you to focus on the present moment. Your investment of time and effort in any of these disciplines will pay huge dividends.

Don't think, however, that you have to "withdraw" from the world and sit all day in the lotus position to surrender your ego. You can still operate a business or engage in sports. The difference will be that you're not looking to establish superiority or to put down anyone. You'll just concentrate on performing to your maximum without worrying about what others are doing.

In case you're wondering, I haven't even come close to surrendering my ego. But I've lightened up on it, I feel a whole lot happier, and things don't get to me like they used to.

It's a paradox—when you surrender your ego, you don't give up anything worthwhile. On the contrary, you *gain* tremendous freedom and improve all areas of your life. You'll find that you have more peace of mind. In addition, you'll feel like a heavy weight (the weight of the ego!) has been lifted from you. Others will interact with you more positively. You'll think more creatively. And you'll respond to stressful situations more effectively.

You'll be happy you made the effort to tame your ego!

35

There's a Lot More Left in the Tube

With ordinary talent and extraordinary
persistence, all things are attainable.

— Sir Thomas Buxton

When I shave each morning, I use shaving cream that comes out of a tube. After using the tube for several weeks, I could see the tube flattening out. I immediately thought, "Can't be much more left in here." I was just about to throw it in the wastebasket when I figured I could eke out another shave or two.

Much to my amazement, the shaving cream kept coming out day after day after day. I ended up getting 19 more shaves from that tube! And to think that I was just about to throw it away.

I'm sure you've experienced the same thing with a tube of toothpaste or shampoo. It looks like the tube is just about empty, but you keep folding the tube and squeezing — and you get days or weeks of extra use from the supposedly empty tube.

There's a lesson here for all of us. We work toward a goal and sometimes get frustrating results for a long time. Things aren't working out as we had anticipated. We think there's not much left in "our tube" and we give some thought to quitting. The reality is that we have a lot more left in the tube, if we'll only continue to believe in ourselves and keep moving forward.

In fact, our biggest breakthroughs often occur when we think there's nothing left in our tube. You see, there's a polarity to life, and when you experience setbacks and disappointments, these are often balanced by significant achievements. Yet most people quit before the "turnaround" happens.

Harriet Beecher Stowe put the principle this way: "When you get into a tight place and everything goes against you until it seems that you cannot hold on for a minute longer, never give up then, for that is just the place and time that the tide will turn."

About 10 years ago, Jack Canfield and Mark Victor Hansen began pitching their book to various publishers. The first 30 rejected their book. They could have thrown in the towel then, believing the tube was empty. Then they got the 31st rejection ... and the then the 32nd rejection. Was the tube empty? They didn't think so. On the 34th attempt, they finally got a publisher to say "yes" to their book. That book was *Chicken Soup for the Soul*, and it spawned a series of books that has now sold over 100 million copies!

Sometimes we have to fight our own doubts as to whether we can keep going in the face of setbacks. At other times, we have to ignore the beliefs of others who tell us that there's nothing left in our tube and that we have to give up on our dreams.

Take the example of George Foreman—businessman, broadcaster and former heavyweight boxing champion. As he approached the age of 40, George decided he would come out of retirement and regain the heavyweight championship. Most people thought he had nothing left in the tube; certainly not enough to win the championship again at his "advanced" age. They said he was too old, out of shape and "rusty" after being away from boxing for so long. But George never listened to the naysayers and on Nov. 5, 1994 at the age of 45, George Foreman knocked out Michael Moorer to recapture the heavyweight title. In the end, it didn't matter that others doubted George because he never doubted himself. He knew he had plenty left in the tube.

Some of you may be wondering whether there's ever a time to "cut your losses" and stop pursuing your goal. I think the answer to that is "yes," but it's usually when you come to the point where you lack enthusiasm to achieve that goal, or if you find you no longer have the commitment to do what it might take to accomplish it. Without enthusiasm and commitment, there really is very little left in your tube.

However, if you're still excited about reaching a goal that may seem off in the distance, it might be time to reexamine your strategy and see if any adjustments are called for. After all, there's no point in continuing to take steps that have proven ineffective.

Once you believe you have a viable strategy, and you're willing to expend the energy and effort to do what it takes to accomplish your goal, don't give up. It's just a matter to time until you'll get a "second wind." If you've played sports or exercised, you've experienced the "second wind." You're exerting yourself for a while and you think you can't go on any longer. Then, you suddenly feel a new burst of energy as you catch your second wind. You're re-energized!

William James said "most people never run far enough on their first wind to find out they've got a second." Don't let that happen to you. What a shame to give up when you can still reach your fondest dreams.

So, when you think the tube is just about empty, take heart and realize that now is not the time to call it quits. Success may be just over the horizon.

36

Goal Setting:
One Size Does Not Fit All

What's important is finding out what works for you.
— Henry Moore

If you've listened to motivational speakers or read any self-help books, you've undoubtedly been told about the importance of setting goals. In fact, many people will tell you that goals are the key to success. Well, I've studied goal setting for nearly 20 years and I have a confession to make: I still don't have a handle on this intriguing subject.

Here's the problem. Motivational speakers and writers frequently oversimplify goal-setting. Those who advocate what I'll call the "traditional goal setting method" advise you to do the following to achieve your objective:

- ◆ Set a goal — in other words, determine what you want to achieve
- ◆ Put the goal in writing
- ◆ Set a time deadline for the attainment of the goal
- ◆ Develop a plan and work the plan
- ◆ Visualize a successful result

- Maintain a positive attitude
- Measure your progress and make adjustments, where needed
- Persist until you reach your goal

All of this sounds great, except for one problem — most people don't achieve their goals using this method! The vast majority fall way short of the mark. I've achieved many goals and also failed to achieve some goals with this system. I'd also bet that virtually all of the people reading this article have failed to achieve many of their goals using this formula — despite the fact that they were positive and took considerable action.

Where did we go wrong? Why do we accomplish some goals using this formula, yet fail to achieve others? While I don't pretend to have all the answers, here are some of my observations on the subject of goal setting.

1. **Many people succeed without having specific goals.** Over the years, I've noticed that there are many high achievers who have succeeded **without** setting goals at all. Actor Harrison Ford has said that he did not have a goal of becoming a movie star. Antonio Banderas said he never sets goals and finds goal setting very limiting. Cindy Crawford never set out to be a "supermodel." Former Secretary of State Madeline Albright said she never set a goal to become Secretary of State — or, for that matter, to be appointed as Ambassador to the United Nations. And, I'm guessing that Vincent Van Gogh did not have a goal reduced to writing that said: "I will paint three masterpieces in the next 90 days and earn one million dollars."

   The bottom line: some people are hugely successful without using traditional goal setting methods.

2. **Whether or not you set goals, you need clarity and passion to be successful.** When I cite examples of those who succeeded without goals, I want to emphasize that these people still had a clear vision of what they wanted to do in their lives. They were and are passionate about their work, they are constantly learning and growing in their field, they are willing to take risks, and they are committed to doing whatever it takes to keep moving forward. People who are vague and uncertain never attain long-term success.

3. **The rules are different when it comes to business and sales.** In business and in sales, I've found that to be successful, you DO need to be a goal setter (using many of the traditional methods). Here's why: in sales, you need to get results quickly.

    Either you produce, or you're "out of the game." Businesses can't afford to take the view, "We'll work hard and whenever we succeed, that's okay." With that approach, the business probably would not meet its payroll and would not gain the confidence of investors. There are some companies that prosper without setting specific goals, but these organizations are very much the exception.

    More and more, businesses are using personality assessments to test applicants for sales positions and to determine beforehand whether the applicants have the potential to succeed in sales. This is a positive approach and helps to identify those who are well suited to play under these "rules."

4. **Some people are simply not suited to traditional goal setting models.** Many people who advocate traditional goal setting methods claim it can work for anyone. I no longer believe that. If Harrison Ford worked as an insurance salesman, he probably would have failed miserably. Some people simply don't

respond well to setting specific goals and achieving them within certain time deadlines. That's not the way they perform at their maximum.

5. **Failed goals usually reveal a lack of commitment.** We have the ability to achieve most of the goals we set. However, we often lack a necessary ingredient: commitment. We think we're committed to achieving a goal, but in reality, we're not willing to do whatever it takes to accomplish the objective. We get frustrated and eventually give up the goal. So, if you're not making much progress on a goal, there's a good chance that you're not really committed.

6. **Failed goals serve a purpose.** It's easy to look at failed goals as a disappointment or as a bad thing. I don't see it that way, however. In fact, "failed" goals serve a purpose—to re-direct us to a better path. Often, we set goals based on what others tell us to do—or what seems like a good way to be successful or make money. When we don't achieve these goals, we give up on them and then have an opportunity to pursue a different path, which is often more in line with our abilities and our unique personalities.

7. **There is an "X" factor when it comes to attaining goals.** Sure, you need a positive attitude, enthusiasm and commitment to achieve a goal. But there's also an intangible factor working behind the scenes—I call this the "X" factor. As we've all seen in sporting events, the championship game can be decided by a bounce of the ball, a fraction of an inch or a missed call by a referee. Granted, it's the prepared competitor that puts himself or herself in a position to win, but make no mistake about it, sometimes serendipity or fate seems to step in to help us achieve certain goals.

More than 40 years ago, Maxwell Maltz, M.D., wrote a classic book on goal setting entitled *Psycho-Cybernetics*. Dr. Maltz believed passionately that we need to have goals or targets. However, he thought it was counterproductive to try to figure out with the conscious mind how to attain the goal. He recommended focusing on the end result and allowing your automatic guidance system to determine the "means whereby" that goal is achieved.

My point is that goal setting is not a "one size fits all" concept. If I've confused a bunch of people here, that's okay. If you out and out disagree with me, that's fine, too. I want you to start thinking more about goal setting instead of simply following methods that don't work for you. Traditional goal setting methods work for some people, and I would encourage those people to continue using them. But they don't work for everyone, and the statistics prove that very convincingly.

There is a path that will work for you. Keep challenging and fine tuning the various approaches to goal setting and you'll find a system that will produce positive results for you!

37

More Discipline, More Success

For every disciplined effort there is a multiple reward.

—Jim Rohn

When you hear the word "discipline," you may think about being scolded by a parent or teacher. Or perhaps you think of the rigid procedures followed by the military. Discipline certainly doesn't sound like much fun, and definitely carries a somewhat "negative" connotation for most.

Those who succeed, learn and grow, however, see discipline quite differently. They recognize that discipline is truly an ally ... a vehicle that allows us to achieve the results we want to attain.

Let's take a closer look at the meaning of this word. The dictionary definition of discipline is "training of the mind, or body, or the moral faculties; self-control."

Discipline is really about forming and sticking with certain beneficial habits or routines, while curtailing those actions that are inappropriate or might ill-serve us. Whether or not we care to admit it, we're all creatures of habit. Every day, we're training our minds and bodies to get certain results. You may not like the results you're getting, but you've developed a training program to produce those results. The habits we follow day in and day out dictate the success we achieve, the way we relate to others, the state of our health, and many other conditions.

Here are some of the ways in which discipline operates in our lives and how we can use this powerful principle to our advantage:

Discipline produces positive results. People who want to save money can achieve that goal. People who want to lose weight can lose weight (in the absence of a medical condition). People who want to build aerobic capacity or muscle strength can accomplish that if they do certain things regularly. That's the beauty of discipline. If you put in the effort, you will produce the positive result you're looking for. It may take you longer or shorter than other people, but you'll get significant results if you keep at it.

Discipline teaches patience and perseverance. If you're out of shape and begin a walking regimen, you may be able to walk a half-mile the first day. The second day you walk a half-mile and one block. The third day, you walk a half-mile and two blocks. You're excited to be making progress each day, but you realize that it will take some time before you can walk five miles. You're learning that most goals take time, and that there are no overnight successes. Too many people nowadays are seeking the "quick fix." Disciplined activity teaches us to be patient and to realize that "slow and steady" wins the race.

Discipline is "contagious" and builds momentum. When you make the commitment to follow a particular discipline, you're going to be thrilled with the results you get. If you're on a diet and lose ten pounds in the first two weeks, you'll be motivated to continue. If you put aside 10% of your money from each paycheck into a savings account, you're going to get a feeling of satisfaction from watching that account grow. But there's a further bonus as well. After you make considerable progress in one area, you'll be sold on the power of discipline. You'll want to make positive changes in other areas of your life. You may decide to join Toastmasters to improve your speaking ability or sign up for classes to enhance your technology skills.

Discipline enhances self-esteem. I've seen it happen countless times. You start to exercise and you have more energy and lose weight. You feel better about yourself. There's an added confidence, more spring in your step. With added self-esteem, you look better. You have more energy. You project confidence and attract many positive things into your life.

As you've been reading this article, I'm guessing that something is jumping out at you—the area where you need to get some discipline! Maybe you need to follow a system to contact new prospects more consistently. Perhaps you need to establish a budget and eliminate impulse purchases. Or maybe you need to start exercising and get into better shape.

I'm not promising you that it will be all fun and games. Discipline gets results but it isn't always fun. I'm always amused when I listen to Jack LaLanne (now in his 90s) being interviewed about his incredible physical condition. When asked if he loves exercising every day, he says with a smile, "I hate it." But Jack does his routine every day because he loves the **results** he gets from doing those daily exercises.

Julie Andrews expressed the value of discipline this way: "Some people regard discipline as a chore. For me, it is a kind of order that sets me free to fly." It's time for you to be free to fly and to realize your greatness.

Determine the most important discipline that would enhance your life. You know, the thing you always say you're going to do "some day." There's no better time to start than right now!

38

Loosen Your Grip on Worry

Worry is as useless as a handle on a snowball.
— Mitzi Chandler

On an intellectual level, you know that worry does a lot more harm than good. When you worry, your muscles tighten. Your body aches. Your energy is drained. Charles H. Mayo said that "worry affects the circulation, the heart, the glands and the whole nervous system." Worse yet, your worrying does absolutely nothing to change the conditions you're worrying about!

That said, here's some encouraging news: you can learn to loosen your grip on worry. What follows are some techniques for reducing the amount of time you spend worrying:

1. Don't fight worry. This is a battle where worry is going to win in the end. There's an old saying, "What you resist, persists." Have your ever said to yourself, "I shouldn't be worried" or "I've got to stop worrying?" Well, did it calm you down? No. You tried to resist worry, and it persisted. Telling yourself not to worry is like telling yourself not to think about a zebra. (What did you just think of?)

2. **Recognize that worry is a choice you make**. When you look at worry as a choice, you'll be taking an important step in reducing the amount of time you worry. A part of you will begin to think, "Why would I ever continue to worry if I had a choice in the matter?" You may not think of worry as a choice because you developed the habit of worrying many years ago. You've trained your mind to worry in response to certain stimuli. Fortunately, you can develop a new habit. You can teach your mind to act in a more constructive way such as being focused in the present moment or concentrating on something positive.

3. **Clear your mind**. There are certain disciplines that enhance peace of mind and reduce worry and tension. Some of them are: meditation, yoga, Zen, tai chi and various martial arts. You can also clear your mind through prayer and by releasing your worries to a Higher Power. I can personally attest to the calming effect of yoga, having taken classes for the last seven years. Yoga postures and relaxation exercises keep you in the present moment and open up certain tension areas in the body. Meditation also allows you to let go of worry thoughts and to focus on the present moment, where there are no worries. (While worrying, you are concentrating on what may happen in the future.) Most people do not take advantage of these disciplines because they involve effort and they take time to learn. I suppose it all depends on how much you want to give up worry and enjoy peace of mind.

    You can also clear your mind with physical exercise. I'm sure you've experienced this feeling of well-being many times. You had a difficult day and you were worried about a lot of things. You went to the gym or took a brisk walk. After your exercise session, your mind was calm and at ease.

4. **Prepare or take some constructive action.** Often we worry about how we're going to perform a certain task. For example, we have to make a speech and we're concerned about how the audience will respond. Instead of worrying, here's a better approach: spend time preparing for the speech. The more you practice and prepare, the more confident you'll become ... and the less you'll worry.

5. **Breathe**. When you're worried, your breathing becomes very shallow and your body is tense and uncomfortable. Whenever you feel worried, take some slow, deep breaths and you will feel calmer right away.

6. **Limit your exposure to the media.** We are under attack ... from the media! This barrage of negative news is enough to make anyone worry. It has gotten to the point where you can put on any news channel and hear about murders, terrorism and catastrophes 24/7. There are panels of people discussing every potential catastrophe they can imagine. 99.9% of these gloom and doom scenarios will never happen, and yet they bombard our minds with this poison. Do you really need to hear that stuff? How is it helping you? You'd be hard pressed to find any stories that increase your peace of mind or have any positive aspect. You can get the news you need in a few minutes. Then shut off the TV! (Newspapers and radio aren't much better, by the way.)

7. **Cut yourself a little slack**. We often worry that things won't go exactly as we want. We expect perfection and then struggle to somehow reach that ideal. If you continue with that approach, you'll always be worrying because you're creating a standard you can't consistently maintain. If you're doing the best that

you can, let that be enough. Nobody lands the sale every time ... nobody hits a home run in every at-bat ... and nobody makes a flawless presentation each time. Be content with excellence and stop worrying about being perfect.

8. **Hang around people who don't worry.** These people really exist, and it's worth finding them. When you're in the company of calm people, you'll feel calmer. Furthermore, you can ask how they're able to avoid worrying. You can then decide which of their strategies are appropriate for you.

Mark Twain once said, "I have spent most of my life worrying about things that never happened." There's no question that worry makes you sick and doesn't produce any beneficial results. Yet, I don't think worry is a habit you can change overnight. Rather, it's a subtle shift in where you place your attention. You loosen your grip on worry gradually. You can discipline your mind to spend more time in the present moment or on something positive. It's well worth the effort and your body, mind and spirit will thank you for it.

39

You're Allowed to Say "No!"

*I don't know the key to success but
the key to failure is trying to please everybody.*

— Bill Cosby

You've got more work than you can possibly handle. Not to mention the time you're spending as an officer of your trade association ... and as coach of your child's soccer team. Your phone rings and it's Sally, another officer of the trade association. Sally tells you what a great job you're doing for the Association and then asks if you'd be willing to chair the Committee putting on a large event in three months.

You know this project will involve countless hours of work, including weekends. You get a sinking feeling in the pit of your stomach. Your heart tells you to say "no." Your spirit tells you to say "no." But somehow, what comes out of your mouth is "Yeah, I'll do it."

What happened here? How did "no" turn into "yes?" Maybe you didn't want to let others down. Or, perhaps, you wanted to be liked. For whatever reason, you agreed to do something that you didn't want to do. For most of my life, I lived this way. Saying "yes" when I really wanted to say "no." I'll bet you've done the same thing many times.

This can happen at work when someone asks you to take on an extra task, or to help out on the weekend. And in our leisure time, we also have to make decisions when it comes to family, community and other activities.

I know what some of you are thinking. If I say "no" to some of these things, I'm going to look bad or hurt my chances for a promotion. For example, if I decline a request from my supervisor, I'll be viewed as someone who isn't loyal to the team. If I say "no" to attending my cousin's wedding (the cousin I haven't seen in 15 years), the rest of the family will be talking about me.

Yes, there ARE consequences to saying "no." You might not get the promotion. Your relatives might talk about you behind your back. But let's not kid ourselves here. There are also consequences to saying "yes" when you don't want to say "yes." You become resentful and angry. You feel that you're not in control of your own life. You're not living a life that's consistent with your values and priorities.

I'm not encouraging you to become lazy and refuse to go the extra mile at work and in your personal life. We all do activities that we don't particularly enjoy, like working through lunch on a key project or attending a wake after a long day at work. Furthermore, this isn't about being selfish and thinking only of your own interests. But I'm here to say that YOU count, too! And you block your own success when you feel resentful about doing things you don't want to do. Unwanted activities are not only time consuming; they drain your energy.

So, what can you do to help you say "no" instead of "yes?" It's very helpful to set boundaries, because that will help dictate your answer when someone asks you to do something. Even better, let people know about these boundaries beforehand so they won't be taken by surprise when you say "no." For instance, if you resolve that you won't work on weekends (except in certain limited, emergency situations), when someone asks you to help out on Saturday, you can decline and tell them you spend weekends with your family. For me, my exercise time on Saturday and Sunday is sacred. If I'm not doing a weekend presentation or traveling, it takes a lot for me to cancel or re-schedule my exercise sessions. If someone asks me to do something during those times, I will politely say "no" because I value my health and well being too much to let other things get in the way.

I also get numerous requests to speak at certain service clubs and trade association meetings on weekday nights. I am honored to be asked, but in most instances, I will politely decline. I set some boundaries and decided that I will do a certain number of these presentations each year, but that's it. Otherwise, I won't be able to spend quiet time at home in the evenings. If anyone thinks I'm being unreasonable, that's okay. I feel better about the decision I've made because I'm being true to what's important in my life. As a result, I've found that my presentations are more authentic and effective.

You might think that you're indispensable ... that you have to say "yes" because the world will fall apart if you don't run to the rescue each time. What nonsense! In the end, you let yourself down and wind up feeling hurt.

Here's the bottom line: You're allowed to say "no." It's a small two letter word with the power to liberate you and significantly improve the quality of your life.

40

Recognize Others
and Build Your Success

*The deepest principle in human nature is
the craving to be appreciated.*

— William James

Do you like to be recognized and appreciated for your efforts? I do. When someone calls or writes to tell me how he or she benefited from my articles or presentations, I feel great. I also remember that person and find myself wanting to help that individual in any way that I can.

If, as William James suggests, humans "crave" appreciation, one might expect that people would always be expressing appreciation to others. Yet, I find that this is not the case. Few people take the time to call or send a letter to recognize another person's efforts. When people receive poor service or are mistreated in any way, they are quick to register a complaint. But when these same people receive excellent service or are treated especially kind, they seldom offer praise.

When you fail to recognize another person who has been helpful, you rob yourself of the satisfaction that comes from expressing appreciation and you rob the other person of the joy that comes from receiving praise and recognition.

If someone refers a client to you, sends valuable written materials, or otherwise assists you in your business or personal life, send an e-mail or a handwritten note of thanks. In some instances, a phone call is appropriate. The recipient of the note or call will be much more inclined to continue helping you in the future. Why? Because you are satisfying the "deepest principle in human nature" — the need to be appreciated. If a company employee or representative renders excellent service, you might also send a letter to his or her superior, pointing out the special service you received from that individual.

Although you should not offer praise or compliments for the purpose of securing future advantages, you are guaranteed that this practice will work to your benefit. Think about it. If one of your customers wrote to thank you for the superior service you rendered, wouldn't you go out of your way to help that customer in the future?

Let's look at an example. On Monday, Mrs. Jones of ABC Company gives excellent, yet identical service to Customer #1 and Customer #2. Following Mrs. Jones' efforts, Customer #1 says nothing and does nothing. On Friday, Mrs. Jones receives a handwritten note from Customer #2, in which Customer #2 expresses sincere thanks to Mrs. Jones for her competence, courteousness and efficient handling of the order. The next time that Customers #1 and #2 call Mrs. Jones for an order, don't you think that Customer #2 is going to receive just a little bit extra service?

Make It A Habit

When praising or recognizing the efforts of others, make sure that your comments are sincere. People know when you are trying to manipulate them through flattery.

I suggest that you develop the *daily* habit of acknowledging others and praising them for any contribution that they make to your life. For instance, if a coworker has helped you or made your job easier or more enjoyable in some way, be certain to thank that individual for his or her assistance.

Here's another example. If you receive particularly good service from a waiter, tell him at the end of the meal how well he performed his work and how much he contributed to your enjoyment of the meal. His face will light up and you will have a good, warm feeling inside. You might also make a note of how he treats you the next time he has an opportunity to serve you.

If you will make a commitment to develop this habit, you will stand out from the crowd and enjoy more success. In order to succeed, you need the cooperation of other people. Doesn't it make sense that people will be more apt to help you if you recognize and appreciate them? Besides, whether or not you receive any tangible benefits, you will feel better when you acknowledge and praise the efforts of others.

My guess is that right now you can think of several people who have done things for you or assisted you in a special way in your business and personal affairs. Pick up the phone or write them a note immediately and let them know that you do appreciate them. Make this a habit and you'll find that you will get more of the things you want in life.

41

The Attitude Accelerator

A strong passion for any object will ensure success,
for the desire of the end will point out the means.

— William Hazlitt

"How can I build a more positive attitude and maintain it?" That's a question I'm constantly asked. My typical answer is this: you get a positive outlook by disciplining your mind through repetition. You read positive material every day. You listen to uplifting audio programs. You hang around people who are positive. You use positive language.

But there's one more technique you can use to get a tremendous boost in your attitude—I call it the "Attitude Accelerator." What is this magical formula?

Pursuing Your Passion

By passion, I mean an activity that when you do it or even speak about it, you get excited. You come alive. Your enthusiasm bubbles over.

Some people are fortunate enough to be in a career where they pursue their passion each and every day. These are the people who love going to work. Let's face it. If you hate what you're doing all day, it's tough to have a positive attitude.

For the purpose of this article, I'm concentrating on areas where you take an *active* role. For example, you could be passionate about watching sports as a spectator, but that's not what I'm getting at. I'm asking you to identify opportunities where you can participate. It doesn't have to be something where you work up a sweat. You could collect stamps or coins or comic books. You could study art history and visit museums. You could write a book. Only *you* know what gets your juices flowing.

I know what some of you are thinking. You're saying to yourself, "I know what my passion is, but it would be unrealistic for me to pursue it right now. I have a mortgage to pay. I have to help support my family. It's just not possible for me to quit my job and do what I love."

Rest assured, I'm NOT suggesting that you act irresponsibly. You don't have to quit your job to pursue your passion. Lots of people use this as an excuse. The truth is, you can treat your passion as a hobby at the outset. That's what I did. I loved motivational materials so much that I started to think about how I could share this information with others. All I knew was that I was passionate about this material and wanted to do something with it.

I was still a practicing attorney at the time. I was also someone who never took risks, who always played it safe. I certainly didn't see how I could work this into my life. Then I got an adult education catalog in the mail at home, describing night courses being given at the local high school. In the back of the catalog, there was a page that said, "Are you interested in teaching a course? If so, let us know your area of expertise and send us an outline." I submitted an outline, and much to my surprise, I got a call that the outline was approved and my class would start in a few months.

Since the course was at night, I was able to teach after working my regular day job as an attorney. It was one of the best decisions I ever made and it opened up a whole new world for me. I'm not telling you this story to pat myself on the back. The point here is this: you can keep working at your regular job and still follow your passion. I actually treated my passion as a hobby for five years while phasing out my legal career.

Let me share another example. David Baldacci was a lawyer with a wife and two children. Yet he had a passion to be a writer. Between 10pm and 2am every night, he worked on his writing. He had fun doing this—it wasn't a chore. He did this for 10 straight years and completed some short stories and screen plays. His sales during this period: ZERO. Then, in 1996, he received millions of dollars for the literary and movie rights to his thriller *Absolute Power*. Clint Eastwood starred in the movie. Baldacci has gone on to write many other best-selling novels. By following his passion and keeping a great attitude, his efforts paid off, big-time.

I'm guessing most of you have a passion you're not following right now. Maybe you want to be a writer. Maybe you'd like to sing, perform in a band, or do stand-up comedy. Perhaps you have talent working with your hands or you're a great cook with some unique recipes. You just know that when you think about, speak about or actually **do** this activity, you feel passionately alive. Time seems to pass quickly. You're completely absorbed and in the moment.

I think every person comes to this earth with special talents to express. You have talents that you bring to the table and you express that talent in a way that nobody else does. You feel positive, fulfilled and happy when you express the talent and you feel like "something is missing" when you refuse to engage in that activity and keep ignoring it. Nature does not give you the desire to do something that you don't have the ability to do. You have the desire to purse this passion because it is something you were meant to develop—and more often than not, when you develop this talent and express it, you're going to make a positive contribution to the lives of others as well.

Following my passion led to a career change. But that isn't the case with everyone. You can have lots of fun and enjoyment pursuing your passion while remaining in your current line of work. In fact, you'll find that your enthusiasm carries over to your full-time job.

That's why I keep saying that you don't have to quit your job. Put that excuse to bed. Find *some* way to do what you love. Take the time you've been watching TV or reading the negative articles in the newspaper and re-allocate it to pursuing your passion.

By the way, just because you're passionate about doing something doesn't mean you'll be able to do it well right away. In most instances, you have to develop the talent, and be willing to face your fears.

I had a passion for communicating motivational ideas, but at the beginning I had no experience in public speaking. I had to develop that talent over a period of years. I also had to learn to improve my writing skills. The same is true with you. Here again, don't use the excuse that you're not good enough to pursue your particular passion. If you love to sing, but you think you're not good enough, take singing lessons. Sing badly at the beginning, but SING!

When you follow your passion, you'll be much more positive and excited about your life. That will transfer over into other activities as well. And you'll be amazed at how opportunities open up for you. I'm not saying your passion is guaranteed to make you a lot of money. It may, but then again it may not. In any case, don't have money as your primary focus. You'll be a happier, more fulfilled person when you follow your passion. And, take it from me, it's a decision you will never regret, and it will do wonders for your attitude.

42

Success:
Expect the Unexpected

You have to take risks. We will only understand the miracle
of life fully when we allow the unexpected to happen.

— Paulo Coelho

arly in 2005, I received an e-mail from a Japanese
translator named Takashi. Takashi had translated my
first book, *Attitude is Everything*, into Japanese. Now,
he wanted me to write a self-help book specifically designed
for the Japanese market.

We decided that I would write a story about a retired
businessman who mentors a young salesman on the principles for success.

The project seemed very straightforward. I would write
the book with some help from Takashi. He would translate
the manuscript into Japanese and submit it to prominent
Japanese publishers. At least one of the Japanese publishers
would agree to publish the book. I would enter a contract
with the publisher and both Takashi and I would be com-
pensated for our work. Of course, in the process, we'd also
be producing a book that would be of great value to readers
in Japan.

So, we followed the plan. I worked on the book with Takashi, chapter by chapter, over the course of two months. When we finished the book, we were both excited. Takashi had a particular Japanese publisher in mind so he sent the manuscript to that firm. They expressed interest in the manuscript but after a few weeks, they decided not to publish the book.

Undaunted, Takashi offered the book to another publisher. They thought the manuscript had promise. However, about two weeks later, they too decided not to publish the book. Takashi sent the book to a third publisher, and we got a third rejection. Then a fourth publisher rejected the manuscript. At this point, our project did not look very promising.

Let me backtrack for just a moment. Shortly after we received the first rejection, I was planning to attend Book Expo America, a large annual trade show for the publishing industry. The show was in New York City during the first week of June, 2005. About one week before Book Expo, I was speaking with my friend (and fellow author) Jim Donovan. He told me that the Managing Director of a Japanese literary agency would be attending the show — and he gave me the email address where I could contact this individual. I sent him an email and he promptly responded. We set up an appointment to meet in New York City.

During our meeting, I talked to him about the manuscript I had just written with Takashi. He thought the book had promise and said he would submit the manuscript to Japanese publishers. Right as we were about to part, he said, "I know a South Korean literary agent who I think might be very interested in this manuscript. Do you mind if I show it to him?" Of course, I encouraged him to send the manuscript to this agent.

While all this was happening, events were unfolding in Japan. When Takashi got the rejection from the fourth publisher, he suggested that we revise the book by removing the story and dialogue — and create a book of 57 short essays. The revised book would contain much the same content, but without the story. At this point, I did not know what to think. Takashi was willing to do the diligent work of revising the manuscript and he went on to compile a book of 57 short essays.

Shortly after the revised book was completed, I got an email from the literary agent in South Korea. He had found several publishers who were interested in acquiring the rights to the original manuscript! We selected an excellent Korean publisher and the deal was completed.

At about the same time, Takashi submitted the revised manuscript to the first Japanese publisher that rejected the original manuscript. After carefully reviewing the book of essays, the Japanese publisher agreed to publish the book!

Thus, I started out to write one book for Japan. After a few months, it appeared that the book would not be published in Japan and that a promising project had reached a dead end. Yet, in the end, I have two books being published — one in South Korea and one in Japan. I tell this story not to impress you with my book deals. (Trust me, John Grisham and Stephen King are not jealous.) It's simply an example of how success unfolds in ways we never imagined. Here are a few lessons from this story that apply to whatever goal you've set out to accomplish:

- **Trust your sustained, positive feelings**. When I was writing the book with Takashi, I enjoyed the process immensely. Not only did we like working together, we were able to educate each other on the nuances of our cultures. I have learned that when you experience positive feelings while engaged in an activity, it is a sign that you are on the right course and will eventually achieve positive outcomes. Thus, when challenges and obstacles arose later, I looked back to the positive feelings I had throughout the writing of the book and maintained confidence that this project would be successful in the end.

Furthermore, even if the book deals had not come through, my time would not have been "wasted." By participating in this project, I honed my writing skills. I learned about Japanese culture. And, most importantly, I spent time doing something I enjoyed. How can you call that a "failure?"

[Note: the word "sustained" in this bullet point is very important. One could get temporary enjoyment from abusing alcohol, taking drugs or overeating. However, the "good" feelings are short-lived and are eventually replaced by negative feelings and/or physical discomfort.]

- **Adversity often precedes victory.** As described above, Takashi and I did not enjoy "smooth sailing" on this project. We felt very confident at the beginning that the original manuscript would meet with approval in Japan. But it didn't turn out that way. Instead, we encountered numerous rejections and ran into what seemed like a dead end. However, on the heels of those disappointments, I was referred to the Korean literary agent who found several Korean publishers eager to acquire the rights to the original manuscript. In addition, Takashi came up with the idea of creating a book of short essays and the rights to the revised manuscript were quickly sold to a prominent Japanese publisher.

- **Everything happens for a reason.** A person from Japan who I've never personally met (Takashi) contacts me by email about collaborating with him on a book. Just days before a trade show in New York City, I learn from my friend Jim Donovan that the managing director of a Japanese literary agency will also be attending that event. The managing director decides to refer me to a literary agent in South Korea, who almost immediately gets me a book contract with a Korean publisher. Takashi revises the manuscript and submits it to the publisher who rejected the initial manuscript. This time, they decide to purchase the Japanese rights to the book.

Maybe all of these seem like random "coincidences" to you, but I don't believe that for a minute. There are forces in the universe that conspire to help us, creating opportunities and placing people in our path. We often overlook the significance of these events and these people. As you begin to trust that these events are happening for a reason, you'll be able to take advantage of seemingly random occurrences and use them to your advantage.

Have there been times when you thought success would come to you in a certain way? Here's the reality: in many instances, the people you expect to help you won't. Those you least expect to assist you may play a vital role. Success has many twists and turns. You'll need persistence AND flexibility on your journey. Keep the faith, and trust that you'll achieve a successful outcome.

43

Unclog Yourself

When a wise man is angry, he is no longer wise.
— The Talmud

Think back to the last time you cleaned out piles of stuff in your garage or in your basement ... or when you removed clothes from your closet that you hadn't worn in years. How did you feel after you finished those tasks? I'll bet you felt a rush of adrenaline and a true sense of accomplishment. You walked away from the job feeling more positive about yourself and the rest of the day. Just as a plunger unclogs your sink, cleaning out your physical clutter unclogs you.

When our physical surroundings are cluttered, we feel clogged and uncomfortable both in our physical space and in our consciousness. Our energy is blocked. Our creativity is squelched.

Action Step #1

Roll up your sleeves and start reducing the physical clutter.

If you're like most people, you have clutter in your home or apartment, and you have clutter in your work space. Let's start with your living area. Give away the things you're not using. Consider whether a family member, friend or charity could use each item. Here is my rule to keep clutter in check: if I am going to take IN an item, then an existing item must go OUT. At work, clean up your desk area. Keep on the desk surface only what is absolutely necessary for day to day work. File it or discard the rest. If you have trouble tackling this task, hire a professional organizer who will help you reduce clutter and set up systems to deal with papers and other items. You don't have to become a neat freak. It's about making a significant dent in the clutter that is clogging you! Note: putting your existing clutter in neat piles doesn't count. Our mission is to *reduce* the clutter.

Action Step #2

Forgive those who you feel have wronged you.

Physical clutter is not the only the thing that can clog our system. We remain emotionally and spiritually clogged when we hang on to grudges, resentments and other negative emotions. Are you holding any resentment toward anyone right now? If so, your emotional and spiritual system is clogged. You're devoting energy to that resentment, which "steals" energy you could be applying to more productive things.

You're probably saying, "But you don't know what this person did to me!" That's true, I don't know. What I **do** know is that your resentment or grudge is doing YOU no good at all. Why hang on to something that makes you feel angry and miserable?

If you think your grudge is too hard to give up, consider what happened to Victoria Ruvolo in November, 2004. She was driving her car on Long Island in New York. A 17-year old teenager in another car flung a 20 pound frozen turkey out of the rear window and into the path of oncoming traffic. The turkey smashed the windshield of Victoria's car, with a force that bent her steering wheel and shattered every bone in her face. Surgeons had to rebuild her face with metal plates and screws.

In August of 2005, the teenager pled guilty to second degree assault. Victoria Ruvolo was in the courtroom that day. She had asked the District Attorney to recommend a lenient sentence for the young man. As a result, he received a sentence of only six months in jail. As the young man walked out of the courtroom, she embraced him and comforted him while he was sobbing. She forgave him for a senseless act that almost took her life and which had inflicted devastating injuries.

By forgiving the young man, Victoria Ruvolo got unclogged. She recognized that bitterness would only hurt her as she tried to get on with her life. Her act of forgiveness also helped to unclog the young man's life.

It may be possible to understand how Victoria forgave the teenager since he didn't *intend* to cause severe harm to her. His conduct was reckless, but he didn't set out to hurt anyone. But what about a case where the harm is intentionally inflicted? New York City Police Detective Steven McDonald faced this situation in July of 1986. While on patrol in Central Park, the then 29-year-old detective stopped some teenagers to question them. While he was speaking to them, one youngster (15 years old) took out a gun and shot Steven McDonald in the head and neck. In the hospital, McDonald learned that he would be paralyzed from the neck down for the rest of his life. He needs a machine to breathe.

At the time of the incident, McDonald had been married only eight months and his wife was three months pregnant. He was in the hospital for 18 months. After being released from the hospital, McDonald forgave the young man who shot him. McDonald said he needed to do that to free himself from anger and resentment. Simply put, he needed to get unclogged and to move forward on a mission to change people's hearts.

Steven McDonald speaks in schools about forgiveness and nonviolent conflict resolution. The chances are that whatever happened to you is nowhere near as serious as what happened to Steven McDonald. If he was able to forgive a person who shot him and paralyzed him for life, can you forgive those who have inflicted some type of emotional or physical pain on you?

Remember, you're doing this to unclog *yourself*, so it doesn't matter if the other person accepts your forgiveness or even knows about it. For that matter, the other person could be dead. Forgive the other person and free yourself. Think about family members, friends, colleagues or co-workers. What resentments are you holding onto? These include the major resentments as well as the petty ones. Give up the bitterness and get on with your life. This is not always easy and there is no formula that applies to everyone. Make the important decision to release your negative emotions.

As you reduce physical clutter and forgive those you resent, you'll gain a host of benefits. You'll feel more comfortable in your physical surroundings. Your health will improve. You'll feel less stress. You'll see new opportunities. Your whole life will open up in ways you never imagined.

44

The Key to Your Security

Your future depends on many things, but mostly you.
— Frank Tyger

There's a lot of talk these days about the lack of security in the workplace, especially in corporate America. Events such as downsizing, restructuring, mergers and acquisitions have many workers wondering whether the job they have today will be there tomorrow. This uncertainty has, in some places, resulted in a loss of morale and an unwillingness for some employees to give their best. After all, they think, "If I could be gone soon or have my job radically changed, why give 100% to this organization?"

But, while it's true that the days of working for a company for 30 years, getting a gold watch and a secure retirement package are long gone, the person who suffers most when you don't give your best is YOU!

Why? To begin with, excellence is a habit that cannot be turned on and off like a faucet. We are creatures of habit and either we have a commitment to do the best job we can ... or we condition ourselves to put forth less than our best efforts. Whichever approach we take, it will not be easy to change. Don't make the mistake of thinking that you can withhold your talents and enthusiasm today, then give your all tomorrow.

To illustrate, consider one of your daily habits — how neat you keep your bedroom. If you're the type that throws shirts and pants on top of a chair (or on the floor), how difficult would it be for you to change that habit and fold all of your clothes and neatly put them away in a closet or drawer? I'll bet that you'd find the new pattern almost impossible to follow. Within a day or two, you'd probably take your socks and throw them on the chair, just as you did before! The same is true of the way you approach your work. You either make the commitment to do an excellent job, or you develop a pattern of doing just enough to get by.

That's why, if you're looking for security in a **job**, you're looking in the wrong place. There is no security in *any* job. The security lies **within you**. The key to developing your security is by becoming excellent at what you do, and by continuing to improve your skills. Add to that a very positive attitude and an ability to work well with others ... and, *voila*, you have job security!

When you put forth 100% effort, people notice. You may not be rewarded immediately but you are building a reputation that will serve you well in your current organization, and in any other place you may work in the future.

The bottom line is this: *giving less than your best effort in your current position can only hurt you.*

So, if you want to obtain real security, ask yourself these questions:

- *Do I enthusiastically give my very best at work every day?*
- *Do I cooperate with others and support their efforts?*
- *Do I maintain a positive attitude?*
- *Am I learning to be better at what I do?* and
- *Am I developing the skills that will be important in my field in the future?*

Answer these questions and re-evaluate yourself on a regular basis. When you can finally reply with a resounding, "YES!," you'll have the type of job security that no one can ever take away from you.

45

Call "Time Out"

If you do not change direction, you may end up where you are heading.

— Lao Tzu

In a basketball game, when things are going poorly and the coach doesn't like the way his team is performing, he instructs his players to call a "time out." At this point, the game is stopped for a few minutes while the coach huddles with the team to discuss adjustments needed to get the players back on track and performing more effectively. Of course, during the time out, the coach also points out what the players are doing *right* — which helps to reinforce their positive behavior.

Here's the question: How often in *your* life do you call a "time out" to review what is working for you and to put an end to what isn't? Probably not often enough. Unfortunately, we tend to become entrenched in habits that are not moving us in the direction of our goals. Life is continually providing feedback, however. And it's up to you to become aware of these useful clues — to learn from the results you're producing and to make any changes that may be necessary.

Common Stumbling Blocks

What follows are some common stumbling blocks that prevent us from attaining the success we desire. *When calling a time out, look to see if you are:*

1. **Lacking clarity about what you want.** Your mind is a goal-seeking mechanism and responds best to *specific* targets and pictures. Vague wishes about having a "more fulfilling" job or earning "more money" aren't effective. You should be able to visualize the end result you want to achieve.

2. **Trying to achieve too much at once.** Having *too many* goals is the other extreme. If you try to tackle five major projects at once, you'll probably fail to succeed at any of them. Spreading yourself out scatters your energy and diminishes your power. Concentrate on one major goal at a time; laser-like focus is a necessary element for success.

3. **Not taking enough action.** Most significant achievements take considerable effort. You can't just sit back and hope that success comes to you.

4. **Stubbornly sticking with a losing strategy.** Let's assume that you are trying to market your product or service and you've implemented Plan A. After three months, Plan A is yielding very disappointing results, with no signs of improvement. Examine why Plan A isn't working and develop a *new* plan. This sounds obvious, and yet many people stick with unsuccessful strategies.

5. **Not taking advantage of the knowledge of qualified people.** While "trial and error" sometimes works, you'll waste a lot of time and resources in the process. Instead, you can get back on course quickly

by seeking help or advice from someone who has achieved what you want to achieve. Remember to ask *qualified* individuals — not a friend or relative who knows little or nothing about solving your particular problem.

6. **Hampered by limiting beliefs.** If you are dominated by negative thoughts, you can't possibly produce positive results on a consistent basis. Who controls what you think about? You do. Develop the mindset that you are *unstoppable!*

7. **Lacking positive inputs.** To sustain your positive beliefs, you need frequent positive reinforcement. Read inspiring literature, listen to motivational audio programs, and surround yourself with enthusiastic, upbeat people. That's the environment in which you will maintain optimism and perform at your best.

8. **Refusing to confront the problem.** You've waited five years and your problem hasn't solved itself. Will you wait another five years, hoping that things will turn out differently? *Things don't change unless you change.* It may be that you have to confront your situation head-on, even if this choice will cause some temporary pain and hardship. Your other option — do absolutely nothing and continue to live with your problem.

9. **Trying to skip rungs on the ladder.** In our excitement to reach bold objectives, we sometimes delude ourselves into believing that we won't have to climb the ladder of success in increments. Instead, we think we can immediately soar to new heights. When this doesn't happen, however, we get discouraged. You need to remember that, as Zig Ziglar often says, "the elevator to success is out of

order. You have to take the stairs." So, be patient and set realistic intermediate goals. After all, *success is achieved one step at a time.*

It makes no sense to just bull ahead doing the same things and expecting your results to change. Live your life *consciously.* Examine what's working and what isn't. Then make the necessary adjustments.

Here's an idea: Why not call time out *right now* — then step back onto the court with powerful new strategies for achieving your goals!

46

Let's Make Courtesy More Common

If a man be gracious and courteous to strangers, it shows he is a citizen of the world, and that his heart is no island, cut off from other lands, but a continent that joins to them.

— Francis Bacon

Courtesy. I see less and less of this precious resource each year. It's not yet on the endangered species list, but I *am* concerned. I'm afraid "common courtesy" just isn't very common these days. As we become a more complex, faster moving society, politeness and consideration for others seems less prevalent. And we're all guilty at times.

But, let's face it. Don't you still prefer to do business with those who are polite and considerate? Here are some specific suggestions for being more courteous and building more effective business relationships:

1. **Call when you're running late.** We're all busy. Tighter schedules. Unanticipated traffic and plane delays. But there's simply no excuse for not letting others know when you'll be late for an appointment. And the more notice you can give, the better. That way, the other person can re-arrange his or her schedule and do some productive tasks to fill in the time

before your meeting. Time is a precious commodity. So, respect other people's time and they'll have more respect for you. After all, how do *you* feel when you make a 3:00 appointment and someone shows up at 3:45?

2. **When you ask for proposals or materials, make sure to respond.** We all get plenty of "junk mail" every day. I'm certainly ***not*** suggesting that you respond to these unwanted solicitations. But what about those instances where YOU initiate contact with other companies or individuals to ask that proposals or brochures be sent to you? In my view, common courtesy dictates that you acknowledge receiving those materials and let the other party know that they haven't been selected. (Sure, you may feel bad "rejecting" someone. But it's far worse to leave them hanging. A "thanks but no thanks" or even a plain "no" is better than silence simply because it allows the other party to move on to more important tasks.)

Here again, how do you feel when you're asked to send materials about your product and then you never hear from the prospect again? You feel like the other party, at the very least, owes you a response, whether it be a letter, phone call or e-mail, right?

The same holds true when you ask people to apply for a position in your organization. Those who are not selected are entitled to hear from you. You expect those who apply to research your company and submit carefully prepared materials. In some instances, they have taken part in interviews. Show the same courtesy and let them know that a decision has been made.

3. **"Take it easy" when you are rejecting or criticizing someone.** Are we becoming a harsher, more "in-your-face" society? I think so, and it's not a good thing. I'm all for being honest, but there's a sound

argument to be made for "cushioning" critical statements. For instance, if someone at work buys a new outfit and asks you how it looks (and you think it's horrible) what do you say? Would you say, "That's the ugliest outfit I've seen in years?" The courteous response takes into account the other person's feelings. Maybe something like, "It's certainly different" or "unique."

I'm not asking you to "lead people on" or confuse them about where you stand. However, most people are quite fragile when it comes to criticism or rejection, and there's no purpose in being so direct or "truthful" that you "crush" the other person.

Here's another example. Let's say that a college receives an application from someone who clearly doesn't meet the school's standards for admission. Which of these letters do you think should be sent when rejecting the application?

A. "We regret to inform you that we can't offer you a position at this time. We receive applications from many people and can't offer a space to each one. We wish you much success in your future endeavors."

B. "Compared to the other applications we received, yours was a complete joke. What were you thinking about when you applied here? The answer is NO."

Now, the second letter probably expresses the college's feelings more accurately about the applicant. But, in my view, it's downright cruel. As for the first letter, I wouldn't be happy to get that either (and I did receive many of those!), but there *is* a certain politeness to that rejection.

Courtesy is more than just being nice. Courtesy is good business. And, besides, courtesy makes the world a little more pleasant. So, show every human being the respect that he or she deserves. Remember that what you send out is what will come back to you. Let's all work together to make courtesy a little more common!

47

Embrace Change
and Realize Your Greatness

*One doesn't discover new lands without consenting
to lose sight of the shore for a very long time.*

— Andre Gide

C-H-A-N-G-E. For many, the mere mention of the word triggers sweaty palms and a rapid heartbeat. We learn early in life that change is to be avoided and that we should stay within our *comfort zone*—that area of behavior where we feel safe and at ease. "Trying something new" is frequently looked upon with anxiety or even dread. As a result, we'll often stick to familiar but dissatisfying routines, opting for a "known hell" rather than venturing into uncharted territory.

So, what, exactly, are we afraid of? Perhaps that we will fail if we take a different direction or that others will laugh at us or disapprove of our actions. These fears, while formidable, can certainly be overcome.

I've had first-hand experience dealing with major changes. In fact, you wouldn't be reading these words if I hadn't made the decision to leave the practice of law (after 10 years) and become a motivational speaker and writer.

This was quite a leap for me, made all the more difficult because I had resisted change (even minor change) throughout my entire life. There were risks, and the transition was not easy. But, by embracing change, a new world has opened for me — a career which I absolutely love and a lot more joy and satisfaction in my life.

So, am I saying that you must embark upon a change of this magnitude in your life? Not necessarily. Only *you* have *your* answers. It's not essential that you make major transitions immediately. What is crucial is that you be willing to travel new paths, for without that, you will never stand a chance of recognizing your full potential.

I believe that most of you already know what changes would contribute to your success and fulfillment. It's just that you hesitate to make these changes. Again, that's natural. But if you will agree to welcome change into your life, I strongly believe that you will experience the following positive results:

Confidence
Honoring yourself
Adaptability
Newness
Growth
Esteem

Although these positive factors are interrelated, let's examine each one separately.

Confidence. When you confine yourself to a few limited areas, you are telling yourself, "I can't handle anything beyond this." Naturally, your confidence level remains low. On the other hand, when you actively pursue change, you learn that you are capable of doing far more than you thought. No, you won't become a dynamo overnight. But ... as you successfully expand into several new areas, you begin to say to yourself, "If I handled these new challenges, I'll bet that I can also do _____ ."

You can't gain confidence by sitting on the sidelines as a spectator. Become an active participant, accepting life's challenges — and your confidence will soar.

Honoring Yourself. Change invites you to discover who you are and to express the special talents that only *you* bring to this earth. Your real power lies in being true to yourself and in saying "yes" to the unique challenges which life presents to you. Unfortunately, most people listen to the false, self-limiting voice which cautions, "Stay put. Change is risky and you might fail." That message is not the "real" you.

There's another voice inside of you which tells you about your possibilities and beckons you to move forward. When you listen to *that* voice, you tune into your greatness. You are constantly encouraged to make the changes that will bring you happiness and fulfillment. Resist these challenges and you deny the deep and powerful forces within you which are seeking expression. As psychologist Abraham Maslow stated: "If you deliberately plan to be less than you are capable of being — I warn you that you will be deeply unhappy."

Be true to yourself and follow that voice that encourages you to pursue your heart's desires.

Adaptability. Whether you like it or not, change is going to pay you a visit at some point. Suddenly, life will thrust change upon you and throw you for a loop. If you have hidden from change until now, you will be unprepared to handle it constructively. The person who has made it a habit to embrace change, however, is better equipped to deal with the turbulence that life inevitably brings. That person has ridden out the storm before and knows that he or she possesses the inner resources to do so again.

By facing change head-on, you learn how to be flexible and make adjustments. In successfully navigating through change, you also begin to see every change as serving you in some positive way, gaining insight into Napoleon Hill's principle that *in every adversity, there is the seed of an equivalent or greater benefit.*

Newness. Much of the fun and excitement in life comes from experiencing new things. Life can be so boring and dull when you stick to tired, old patterns. Let's assume you had the same thing for lunch four days in a row. On the fifth day, you sit down … and there it is again. The chances are, you wouldn't be too excited. Maybe it's time to shake up things in your life, and to bring back some of the zest you once had.

You'll feel alive and "turned on" when you venture into new areas and face fresh challenges. Routines get boring; change rejuvenates you.

Growth. Unless you embrace change, you won't grow, either personally or professionally. How can you expect to learn and grow if you remain covered up inside your shell? You develop your potential by constantly challenging yourself and expanding your comfort zone. Merely *thinking* about what you might be able to accomplish will get you nowhere. You'll never know the extent of your ability unless you test yourself. You're afraid? So was I. But I learned that backing away from change is a losing strategy which can never have a happy ending. So, take action. You were meant to learn, to grow and to develop your special talents. Yes, you'll take some lumps along the way, but you won't regret your choice to expand your horizons. Eventually, you will find that change and growth are fun, exciting and rewarding. You'll actually begin looking forward to the next challenge!

Esteem. High self-esteem is essential for a successful, fulfilling life — and facing change is guaranteed to increase your feelings of self-worth. On the contrary, when you resist change, you lower your self-esteem and sabotage your success. You are discouraged and feel powerless.

Embracing change causes you to feel good about yourself because you are moving forward in the face of your fears. It doesn't matter what results you achieve right away; the important thing is that you're in the game as an active player. Your self-esteem will continue to grow with each new venture.

Well, then, with all these wonderful benefits just waiting to be yours, why isn't everybody embracing change? In one word: FEAR. Most people are simply too frightened of the unknown. In addition, the process of change is often extremely turbulent, and filled with frustration and setbacks. But that's the price you must be willing to pay. Life rewards those who are willing to be uncomfortable and who press onward with extraordinary faith and relentless persistence.

Now, there is no need for you to take huge risks at the outset. Start with small steps and develop your change muscles gradually, wherever possible. But get to it. You know, I've met many dissatisfied people who resisted change at all costs and now regret it, yet I've *never* met a single person who chose the path of growth and change and later wished they hadn't.

It's up to you.

48

How to Know When
You Have a Great Idea

New ideas pass through three periods:
1) It can't be done. 2) It probably can be done, but it's
not worth doing. 3) I knew it was a good idea all along!

— Arthur C. Clarke

If you're like me, ideas are popping into your mind all the time. In your business, you may be thinking of ways to boost efficiency, develop new products or better serve your customers.

Of course, the hard part is to figure out which ideas should be developed. While this isn't an exact science, there are some signposts we can use to spot great ideas. Here is a checklist to help you the next time you're wondering whether your idea is worth pursuing:

1. **The idea won't leave you alone.** Great ideas excite you and consume you. You just can't get them out of your mind. In the car, you're thinking about this new idea and how to implement it. You're thinking about it before you go to bed — and when you wake up in the morning. This is the first sign that an idea has promise.

2. **You want to discuss it with everyone you see.** Your idea gets you enthused to the point where you want to discuss it with your co-workers, friends and relatives. Now, I'm not saying that all ideas should be discussed openly right away. There are times when ideas should be kept confidential. Only you can make that decision. The key is that you *want* to share this idea with the world.

3. **Some people will reject the idea immediately.** It's inevitable. You're going to share this idea with some people, and they'll reject your idea immediately. You'll hear things like, "it would never work" or "it's been tried before." This is just life's way of testing your resolve. Don't be discouraged. You'll also find some people who offer valuable suggestions that you'll incorporate as you move forward to implement your idea. Welcome these comments.

4. **The idea is a good match for your talents.** Ideas are especially powerful — and likely to be successfully implemented — when they utilize your individual abilities. This is life's message that this idea is especially for you. However, don't use this as an excuse to back away from projects that require you to develop new skills. A great idea will likely make you stretch a bit, even while building on your strengths.

5. **The idea is original.** You know you have a good idea when it's something that nobody else has tried exactly. Originality doesn't mean you invent something completely new. Your new concept might be a 5% change in an existing concept. For example, you may be writing a book on self-development, but you're presenting the concepts in a way that hasn't been done before. Contrast that approach with the dozens of "copycats" who tried to jump on the bandwagon

after the enormous success of the *Chicken Soup For The Soul* books. The idea (a collection of inspiring stories) was not original and the copycats met with little success.

6. **You connect with resources to help you implement the idea.** When you have a good idea and a strong intention to make it happen, what you're looking for begins to look for you! In other words, you start to find articles on the subject that are of help. You suddenly "bump" into people who can offer guidance. This is not a coincidence. The universe is encouraging you to continue.

7. **You see huge possibilities.** I've discovered that the great ideas are the ones that have tremendous upside potential. Of course, there are no guarantees that your idea will pay huge dividends. But when you can envision a phenomenal result — and you just feel it — then you usually have an idea worth pursuing. When you're excited and see huge possibilities, you'll have the persistence to overcome the challenges that will come along the way. And, other people will get caught up in the excitement of your bold vision.

Make no mistake about it. There's a big difference between having a valuable idea and implementing that idea. Lots of people have great ideas but take no action. Once you have an idea that fits the criteria outlined above, take immediate steps to move forward with it. You don't have to be hasty and bull ahead without being prepared. But it's essential that you not let the idea sit. Maintain excitement and momentum by taking proactive steps right away. Your next great idea just might change your life — and change the world!

49

You Have More Control
Than You Think

*The mind is the limit. As long as the mind can
envision the fact that you can do something, you can
do it — as long as you really believe 100 percent.*

— Arnold Schwarzenegger

I arrived at the doctor's office at 7:30 a.m. for a routine check-up and was invited to take a seat in the waiting area. About five minutes later, the doctor's assistant, a young woman who appeared to be in her 20s, called my name and asked me to accompany her to the examining room.

As I entered the room, she smiled and said "Good morning, how are you today?" I responded, "Terrific" and then asked her, "And you?" She replied, *"Good so far, but it's still early."* I'm sure you know exactly what she meant. Nothing had happened **yet** to ruin her day. But she was leaving open the possibility that something negative would occur to change her mood.

I'm not here to criticize this woman. When I was her age, my attitude was a lot worse than hers. Furthermore, I thought precisely as she did — that my attitude was determined by the events that unfolded or the people who crossed my path that day.

Fortunately, about 20 years ago, I began to realize that I had it all wrong. Rather than being *reactive,* I decided to become *proactive.* I took control over my own attitude by reading and listening to positive input every day. Slowly but surely, I gave up the knee-jerk reaction of being negative or frustrated when things didn't go as I pleased. Instead, I was able to make a different choice, regardless of outside conditions. While I wasn't exempt from disappointments, I now had the ability to deal with them more constructively.

What helped drive the point home to me was this: I observed that many people were having a wonderful day even though I knew they were facing challenges. For example, many people in wheelchairs were smiling and happy while others in good health and with full mobility were miserable. Then there were those who were happy even though they had very little money and were fortunate just to have a roof over their heads and enough food to eat, while others with considerable wealth and a lovely home were unhappy because they couldn't afford to buy a larger home.

If you think carefully, you'll come to the inescapable conclusion that people have the ability to **choose** to have a great day, a bad day or something in between. Happiness is indeed a choice. This is something that each person has the power to control, yet only a small percentage of the people in the world exercise this power in a way that serves them.

A Lesson in Dealing with Pain ...

Successful fashion model Petra Nemcova has been on the cover of *Sports Illustrated* magazine. She was on television to promote her book, *Love Always, Petra* (Warner Books, 2005). On December 26, 2004, Petra was on vacation with her boyfriend in Thailand. The two of them were in a bungalow when the devastating tsunami hit. They were thrown into the fierce waves; her boyfriend was swept away and died. Petra clung to a palm tree for 8 hours with a cracked pelvis before she was rescued.

While in the hospital in Thailand, Petra experienced excruciating pain. When she told the doctor how much pain she was suffering, he explained to her that in her mind she was "rating" the pain as "10" on a level of 1 to 10. The doctor suggested that she could just as easily decide that the pain was 4 out of 10 in terms of its intensity. He also told her that she could focus on more positive images and take away much of the sting of the pain. Petra took the advice of the doctor. She no longer rated the pain as a "10" and she focused on more positive things. She reported that the pain was considerably less after she followed this approach. In short, Petra learned that she had significant control over the pain. Relief came not from a pill or an injection, but rather from how she used her mind.

This may sound crazy to some of you. Can you really control the amount of pain you are feeling? Well, consider this: How can certain athletes play with broken bones and other serious injuries, while some of us would claim we couldn't move due to a bruised toe? These athletes have trained themselves to play through the pain, or to ignore the pain altogether. They give themselves a different message. While most of us would say, "I'm hurt and I can't play" the athlete often says, "I have to get out there and help my team to win."

The difference in these responses can't be explained simply by genetics. It's in the way we train ourselves to use our minds, and where we choose to place our focus.

Taking Command

When you become aware of the power of your mind, you've reached the first step in improving the quality of your life. You then need to develop habits that reinforce a positive outlook and positive feelings. Here are some techniques that have worked for millions of people and will work for you:

1. **Saturate your mind with the positive.** Most people saturate their mind with the negative (like watching gossipy TV shows, associating with pessimistic

friends, etc.) and then wonder why they're always in a funk and feeling helpless. Read positive literature every day, preferably in the morning when you wake up. Listen to positive audio programs several times each week, or while exercising. Make sure that you spend time with people who are positive and uplifting. You may need to make significant changes in your regular routine, but that's what it will take to discipline your mind in a positive direction.

2. **Bring gratitude to the forefront.** You maintain a positive attitude and positive feelings when you concentrate every day on the blessings in your life. Everyone gives lip service to gratitude, but it's rare to find a person who expresses gratitude and makes it a priority every single day. The moment you face a challenge, gratitude should come to mind and allow you to realize just how well off you are. No matter what you're facing, I'll bet there are many people who would gladly trade places with you.

3. **Calm the mind.** Today's society is all about rush, rush, rush and go, go, go. When you're caught up in that frenzy, you become tense. Your mind tends to race with unpleasant scenarios and images. The solution is to bring your mind back into the present moment, a place most people rarely visit. You can quiet the mind through disciplines such as meditation, yoga, tai-chi and martial arts. When your mind is quiet, you feel positive and at ease. You're re-connecting to your spirit. Don't make the mistake of thinking these disciplines are not practical. They will help you in your business and your relationships. There is much truth to Blaise Pascal's observation that "all men's miseries derive from not being able to sit in a quiet room alone."

Only you can decide which combination of these strategies will work for you — and how much time you can devote to each practice. That's a matter of personal preference. Do what works for you.

Please understand that I'm not suggesting that you're unaffected by the people who cross your path or the conditions you're facing. Sure, life can be easier when people are cooperative and when you have money in the bank. But life isn't always this rosy. While you can't control all of the circumstances in your life, you can control your *response* to any challenges that come your way. In the end, your outlook is something that *you* decide.

When you've disciplined your mind to be positive, you're going to find that you're happier, healthier and well-equipped to handle whatever happens on the outside.

50

It's Okay to Step Back
Before Moving Forward

It is a rough road that leads to the heights of greatness.

—Seneca

When it comes to success and motivation, there's a lot of talk about always moving toward our goals. Yet, as most of us have learned, the path is not always "full speed ahead" … but rather a journey where we often take a few steps back before re-gaining our momentum.

When I think of people who took quite a few backward steps before advancing, former pro basketball player Bob Love immediately comes to mind. In the 1960s and 1970s, Bob played for the Chicago Bulls and was one of the top scorers in the league, averaging well over 20 points per game. He was a superstar. However, players in those days did not earn the huge salaries earned by today's sports stars. So, after he retired from basketball, he needed to look for a job. But he had a lot of trouble.

You see, Bob Love couldn't talk without stuttering. After years of doing odd jobs, he was hired as a dishwasher and a busboy at Nordstrom's department store, where he was paid

$4.45 per hour. Can you imagine one of today's basketball superstars taking a job as a dishwasher?

Bob performed his job with uncommon care and commitment, working six months in a row without a day off. As a result of his exceptional diligence, he caught the attention of Nordstrom's owner, who paid for Bob to receive speech therapy. Soon after, he returned to the Chicago Bulls to accept the position of Director of Community Relations. Today, Bob Love is one of the top motivational speakers in the world— inspiring people to overcome their setbacks and follow their dreams!

It's hard to imagine anyone taking more steps backward than Bob Love. Yet, by taking this reverse course, he vaulted himself forward to phenomenal success.

Don't think that this principle only applies to athletes or celebrities. A few years ago, I was speaking to my good friend Dave, who lives and works in the Midwest. Dave is a great salesman and was a very successful health club manager in the Chicago area for 10 years. About a year ago, Dave decided to make some changes in his life. He moved to a smaller town in Illinois to "start over" and re-balance his life.

Shortly after moving, Dave was standing on line in a Dunkin' Donuts shop to buy a cup of coffee. At this point, he had no job. Striking up a conversation with a woman who was also waiting, Dave mentioned that he had just moved to the area. The woman told Dave that she owned a restaurant/night club nearby, and offered him a job taking tickets and checking IDs at the door. Remember, Dave was a highly-paid, highly-successful sales manager. He could easily have considered this job "beneath him."

But Dave knew that opportunity often shows up in strange ways. So, he said "Yes" and accepted the offer. The first month on the job, Dave was speaking to a customer in the restaurant and mentioned his prior experience in sales. The customer worked for a large, well-known office furniture company and suggested that Dave apply for a sales position at the company.

Dave applied and was immediately hired. Dave was willing to take a few steps backward and it paid off big time.

Let me share with you one final story—my own. When I made the decision to leave the practice of law to become a motivational speaker and writer, I had to take many huge steps backward before moving forward in a new direction. Part of the price I had to pay was giving up the money, prestige and security of my legal career. Yet, it has been one of the best decisions I've ever made in my life!

We can learn some valuable lessons from these stories:

1. **Opportunity is everywhere and is often found in the "ordinary."** Bob Love's opportunity came after he took a job as a dishwasher. Dave found opportunity on line at Dunkin' Donuts. Too often, we think that opportunity will arrive with fanfare and a marching band to announce it. Just the opposite is the case. Your opportunities will often be subtle and seem quite ordinary. But don't let that fool you!

2. **Be humble and give it all you've got.** Whenever you choose—or are forced—to make a transition in your life, don't let your ego get in the way. We leave one job and feel as if we have to take another that offers the same prestige and the same (or more) money. That's not always our best move. Sometimes the best move is a lateral move ... or a few steps down the ladder. There is no such thing as a job that is "beneath you." Anyone can shine in any job. Bob Love impressed his owner as a dishwasher. Dave stood out from the crowd while checking IDs at the door. I myself began to build a truly rewarding career only after "starting over" as a motivational speaker.

   [NOTE: I'm not suggesting that if you're out of work, you should take the very first job that comes along. However, sitting back and waiting for the "perfect" replacement of your previous job is equally silly.]

3. **Follow your passion and honor your values.** You'll have a much better chance of succeeding if your step "back" involves something you're passionate about—and something that is consistent with your values. In my case, I left a dissatisfying legal career to follow a new path that I was "on fire" about. That propelled me forward. Dave sought to re-balance his life and he moved out in faith to a smaller area to begin anew. Life rewards those who are true to themselves and their deepest desires.

So, the next time you're faced with the possibility of taking a step or two "backward," don't despair. Consider the guidelines discussed here. Your step back may only be a temporary move before you are catapulted to phenomenal success!

51

Let Adversity Lift You
to Higher Ground

The things which hurt, instruct.
— Benjamin Franklin

I t's easy to have a positive attitude when things are going your way. But what happens when you face a problem or difficulty? Does your positive outlook go right out the window? When adversity strikes, most people tend to get discouraged and focus on the negative. This, in turn, leads to more negative thoughts, more negative feelings and, yes, more negative results.

But there's a better way. You see, there's no reason to let your problems destroy your positive attitude. You have the choice to *view your difficulties as opportunities, learning experiences, and challenges for growth.*

Let me acknowledge up front that there may be some of you who have suffered such pain and tragedy in your life that you can't possibly imagine anything positive flowing from that event. It is not my intention to force you to believe otherwise. I do ask, however, that you keep an open mind on this issue.

Every negative event in your life is trying to move you to higher ground — pushing you forward to something better.

It can be as simple as missing your train — and then meeting someone who becomes a new customer.

Many people have heard Napoleon Hill's principle that "in every adversity, there is the seed of an equivalent of greater benefit." It's time to go from an "intellectual" understanding of this concept to actually applying it in *your* life. Here are some guidelines to help you:

1. **Re-wire your brain.** This is a painless procedure and doesn't require pliers or wire cutters! Right now, you may be "wired" to connect *Problem* with "Negative, Gloomy and Bad." It's time to disconnect that circuit. Visualize that wire being cut. You're now choosing to "re-route" the connection from *Problem* to a new circuit that contains "Better Opportunity, Growth, Learning Experience." Once you establish this new connection, you'll be amazed at the difference in your career and in your personal life. When a seemingly "negative" event happens, you'll immediately begin to think, "What's good about this?" And you'll find the benefit!

2. **Don't deny the emotions.** I'm not suggesting that you bottle up your feelings and deny that you're discouraged. This isn't about laughing at funerals or singing when your biggest account calls to terminate the relationship with your company. If you feel like screaming or crying, go right ahead. It's a matter of how long you choose to stay with the negative emotion. In the end, prolonged negative thinking never serves you.

3. **Ask others for examples of how negative situations in their lives turned into positives.** Get ready to hear some amazing and powerful stories! On several occasions, I've had people at my seminars say that being fired was the best thing that ever happened, as

it led them to a more successful career — or to starting their own businesses. I've also had people who
have told me how devastating illnesses caused them
to make important lifestyle changes and to re-order
their priorities.

4. **Take inventory of your "negative" events.** Now, it's
    your turn. In the space provided below, write three
    seemingly "negative" events that have happened to
    you in your life. After listing each one, identify the
    good things that have resulted from that event. Take
    some time with this, even if you don't see anything
    positive right away. Did the negative event lead to
    something better down the road? Did you learn
    anything? Did it give you perspective or make you
    stronger?

Negative Event	Positive Outcomes

Just think of it. You no longer have to choose to get down
when something "negative" happens in your life. Instead of
whining and complaining, you can look for the positive road

that lies ahead. It may take time before you recognize the positive aspect of your situation. But once you put faith in this principle, you *will* find the benefit.

Remember: Adversity is a call to greatness. Not some of the time. All of the time!

52

Make the Most
of Your Opportunities

I will prepare and some day my chance will come.
— Abraham Lincoln

Like many other youngsters, I played Little League baseball. I was a pretty good fielder, but when it came to hitting, I was — to put it bluntly — pathetic. That's because I was afraid of getting hit by the ball. So, when the pitcher reared back to throw, I'd tend to back away from the plate.

One day in my little league "career" stands out in my memory. It was my turn to bat, and I stepped up to the plate to face one of the best pitchers in the league. This kid threw hard. Well, he fired a fastball and I swung. CRACK! By some miracle, I hit the ball and sent a long line drive between the center fielder and right fielder. Let me tell you, I was stunned, never having heard that sound come from **my** bat before. So, I began to race around the bases frantically, chugging as fast as I could. The ball rolled so far that there was no way the outfielder could retrieve it in time. I could have crawled around the bases and made it home safely.

Well, after I crossed home plate my teammates jumped all over me. They, too, were amazed by my slugging prowess.

I was elated ... until, out of the corner of me eye, I saw the catcher from the opposing team walking toward our dugout. He had the ball in his hand ... and he tagged me.

The home plate umpire yelled, "You're out! You missed home plate." Talk about the agony of defeat — not to mention the embarrassment! My home run was snatched away from me. Then, adding insult to injury, the first base umpire said, "He missed first base also." Oh, well. At least, I touched two of the four bases.

How did it happen? Why did I have so much trouble running the bases and completing the home run? My problem was, I didn't *expect* to hit the ball. So, when I did, I wasn't prepared.

You see, when your expectations are low, it's hard to take advantage of "the breaks" that come your way. With that in mind, here are two specific suggestions to help you make the most of your opportunities.

Adjust Your Attitude

When I stepped up to the plate in those Little League games, I had a lousy *attitude*. I kept telling myself, "I'm not a good hitter," and "I'll never hit the ball very far." This became a self-fulfilling prophecy and, as a result, I rarely hit the ball. When I did hit the ball into the outfield that day, I was stunned and ran around the bases like a chicken without a head. Remember, low expectations lead to disappointing results.

Are there any areas of *your* life where you're giving yourself negative messages right now? If so, it's important to change your attitude *immediately*. Otherwise, your performance will remain at a low level.

Be Prepared

A positive attitude, by itself, won't guarantee that you make the most of your opportunities. The next crucial step is *preparation*.

Because I didn't expect to hit the ball, I didn't study the technique for running the bases. (There is a proper technique, you know!) Had I practiced base-running, I would have been more successful when I actually hit the ball.

The same is true in your career. Let's say John is a successful salesperson and has a chance to be promoted to district manager. What kinds of skills might be important for him to develop? First, he'll probably be required to do some public speaking at monthly meetings or sales conventions. If John isn't already an accomplished speaker, he'd do well to join a group like Toastmasters to improve his speaking skills.

John may also need help in motivating and managing a staff with diverse personalities. He can read books, attend seminars and obtain guidance from other successful managers to develop this skill. Regardless of his approach, however, if John fails to prepare, he probably won't make the most of his promotion when it comes; and he may not even land the promotion at all.

By the way, *when* should John start to prepare? As early as possible! The sad truth is, most people start to prepare when it's too late. If John aspires to be a district manager, he should start preparing well before he gets the promotion. That way, he'll demonstrate that he deserves to move up the ladder and, when he gets the new job, he'll be ready to show his stuff!

It all comes down to this: when you combine a great attitude with thorough preparation, you're sure to hit many home runs!

53

Focus on YOUR Attitude

Everyone thinks of changing the world,
but no one thinks of changing himself.

— Leo Tolstoy

After I deliver a presentation about attitude and motivational principles, quite often someone from the audience will approach me to say how much they believe in the importance of attitude. That person will then say something like this: "You know who *really* needs this talk on Attitude? My sister Emily. She's so negative, and I just can't get her to change."

You'd be amazed how often this happens. The names change but the stories are similar. Their husband, their son, their good friend—someone else needs an attitude adjustment. As they speak about their "negative" family member or friend, I can see and feel their frustration.

On the face of it, helping someone become more positive sounds like a very kind and thoughtful, even noble, undertaking. But first impressions can be deceiving. What I've found over the years is that the person trying to "fix" someone else's attitude is doing so for a reason. Sure, they want to help the other person. I don't doubt that. However, there's usually more at play.

Those trying to influence someone else's attitude frequently do so because it creates a *distraction* from their own personal growth journey. In other words, by spending time and energy changing someone else's attitude, you won't have the opportunity to work on your own attitude and growth. After all, you say to yourself, "How can I go out and work on my dreams when I first have to change this other person?"

It's Hard Enough to Change Your Own Attitude

Most people who want to improve their attitude don't develop a dynamic, positive attitude overnight. It takes a little time and a great deal of discipline. Like any new habit, it doesn't feel comfortable at the beginning. I've found that the three most difficult tasks in life are the following:

- Change someone else's attitude
- Change your own attitude
- Remove the cellophane wrapper from a new CD

All kidding aside, try to remember that you don't control the personal growth of another human being. Somehow, we think our mission is to teach the principles of positive living to others so they can lead a better life. And yes, it's true that if others practiced these principles, they would be happier and more successful. Yet we don't get to dictate someone else's thoughts or actions. The other person's life is his or her life—not your life. What you would do if you were "in their shoes" is irrelevant. Each person has dominion over his or her attitude and actions. As I see it, we must respect each person's right to think and act as they please.

You don't need distractions that make your own journey of personal development more difficult. When you're trying to fix someone else's attitude, you're creating obstacles to your success.

Why You Create Distractions

At this point, you might be thinking, "Why on earth would I create a distraction to sabotage my own personal growth?" To put it simply, you're afraid of where your journey of personal growth might take you. When we experience fear, we often back away from the fear to stay in our "comfort zone."

When you begin to develop a better attitude and to explore your potential, a part of you is excited. You're waking up to new possibilities. It's full speed ahead, or so you think. Despite your initial optimism, however, a part of you wonders what will happen to your existing friendships and relationships if you move forward boldly in your life. You speculate (at least on a subconscious level) that some people will not accept the "new" you. Fears arise that you might damage those relationships or even "lose" them. As a result, you seek something to derail your growth—a distraction or project that will keep you where you are.

A part of you also wonders what will happen if you are happier and more successful. What demands will life place upon me? Will I be able to handle my new success? Once again, a fear of the unknown. In response to fear, we often find a way to retreat.

Please understand that this article is not about refusing to help others. It's great to share a positive message, or a book or audio program that you feel will help someone to lead a better life. I would encourage you to keep doing that. It only becomes a problem when the other person doesn't seem open to your gesture or intent, and then you decide that you are going to "convert" this person to a positive way of thinking no matter what it takes! That's when you cross the line into something that won't serve either you or the other person.

A Better Strategy

If you find yourself trying to "convert" other people to a more positive way of living, first acknowledge this. Don't get defensive about it or deny it. Be honest, but also easy on yourself.

Next, re-direct the focus to your own life. Concentrate on the thoughts, feelings, and actions that will move you forward. Accept that at times during your journey you will become afraid, and that change may make you uncomfortable in the short term. Have the courage to confront these fears and to embrace change. You'll find that you have what it takes to overcome these feelings.

When you keep the focus on developing your own attitude—and then put your attitude into action—a strange, wonderful thing will happen. You'll have more influence to affect the attitudes of other people! You see, it is your positive *example* that has the most impact on others. Your words alone will not convince them. But when you practice being positive and confronting your fears, others will see the positive changes in your life...and they will want to know what you're doing so that they, too, can enjoy these same benefits.

54

Take It Personally ...
Then Let It Go

If you have no critics, you'll likely have no success.
— Malcolm X

Several years ago, I read don Miguel Ruiz's best-selling book, *The Four Agreements* (Amber-Allen Publishing, 2001). It's an insightful little book with a message that seems so simple—and yet is so profound. In his book, the author invites the reader to adopt a code of conduct that includes four agreements. In this article, I'd like to focus on the second agreement, which states: "Don't Take Anything Personally."

Great advice, isn't it? But it's easier said than done. The problem is, most of us take criticism or rejection personally. *Very personally.* As I was reading this wisdom about not taking things personally, a story popped into my mind.

Very early in my speaking career, I was hired to give a two-hour presentation to an organization that was having a conference in New Jersey. There were about 250 people in the audience and half of them really didn't want to be there. To make matters worse, I was incorporating some new material into my presentation, material that I had not yet tested before an audience of this size.

Parts of my presentation were well received by the audience. However, some of it did not go over well. At the end of the seminar, I handed out evaluation sheets so I could get some feedback about my performance. Some of the comments were quite positive: "Excellent presentation that really made me take an in-depth view of myself" and "I loved it." So far, so good.

Then, there were the other evaluations. In response to my question, "What are the best, most usable ideas you gained from this program?" one attendee stated, "None." And there was one gentleman who offered this opinion of my presentation: "Join Toastmasters or try some tapes on speaking and presenting." Ouch!

I didn't have a pleasant drive back from New Jersey that day, and I'll admit that I took some of the comments personally. However, by the time I got home, I was able to let it go and to see things much more clearly.

Here are some things to keep in mind the next time you receive harsh comments:

1. **It's not about you.** When people make insulting or vicious remarks to you, it's a reflection of what's going on inside of *them*. The statements are based on *their* emotions, *their* experiences and *their* unique viewpoints. You're simply the target at the moment. Harsh criticism is usually brought on by one or more of the following:

    Ego. Some people will criticize you to boost their own ego. They pull you down a few pegs so that they'll feel superior to you.

    Impatience. Impatient people are also likely to make insulting remarks that are out of proportion to the situation. For instance, if an impatient person feels you should complete a task in 5 seconds—and you take 10—you'll hear something like, "Are you a moron?" Clearly, this has nothing to do with you.

    Childhood Influences. Many people who criticize you without regard to your feelings grew up in an environment where they were criticized harshly and rejected often. They are simply repeating the pattern.

    Accept the fact that people from all of these categories will cross your path from time to time.

2. **Learn from it.** In most cases, you can learn from criticism and rejection. Although the comments may be harsh or exaggerated, there is some truth to be found. For instance, many of the evaluation forms I received from that audience in New Jersey provided excellent suggestions for ways I could improve my seminar. If I simply ignored a lot of the comments that were offered "undiplomatically," I would have lost out on an opportunity to improve.

3. **Laugh about it.** After you get over the initial shock of a critical remark, allow yourself to have a good laugh! It reduces the tension and puts things back in perspective. On the evaluation forms I distributed that day, there was a line that said "May we quote you?" I include this because many people offer positive comments that I like to use as testimonials. In response to this question, the guy who told me to "join Toastmasters" checked "YES" (meaning I was free to quote him). See, sometimes you just have to laugh!

4. **Don't let anyone stop you from pursuing what you want to achieve.** I had a rough day in New Jersey, but I wasn't going to allow a few people to stop me from moving forward and developing my skills. Life will test you to see how serious you are about pursuing a particular path. Sooner or later, you'll face the kind of feedback I got that day in New Jersey. And when you

do, remember: *don't let anyone crush your dream.* If you're doing what you want to do (and aren't hurting anyone else), the only question to ask yourself is: Did I do the best I could in this situation? In New Jersey that day, I gave the best presentation I was capable of giving … at that time. You can't ask yourself to do more than your best.

5. **Cut others some slack.** If there's something I've learned over the years, it's that we have to be a little more considerate of the feelings of others. Sure, we have to provide feedback and criticism at times. But we're all guilty of going overboard, whether to our family or to people at work. We say things that we wouldn't want others to say to us. We get impatient and forget that it took us time to learn the very things we're expecting others to perform perfectly right away.

Don Miguel Ruiz gave some great advice when he said that we shouldn't take anything personally. Yet, I have to admit I'm not quite there yet. What I've done is to limit the amount of time that I take things personally. What I used to take personally for years became months … and then weeks … and then days … and now it's usually measured in terms of hours or minutes. I feel a whole lot better and have achieved a lot more as a result.

Work on reducing the amount of time that you take things personally—and you'll take your life to a new level.

55

Do It Your Way

Do you want to be a power in this world?
Then be yourself.

— Ralph Waldo Trine

"Copycat." It's a word we usually learn in elementary school that always carries a negative connotation. We're criticized for trying to duplicate what someone else has done, instead of being original. As we get older, we tend to use other words to describe imitating others. Perhaps we use the word "conforming." Here again, it usually has a negative connotation.

In the field of self-development, however, many people actually encourage us to "copy" others. Often called "modeling," it is hailed as a very positive trait.

In other words, just do what successful people are doing, and you will be successful. For example, if you're in real estate sales, find someone who is highly successful in that field and do exactly what that person is doing. If you do, the argument goes, you'll enjoy the same success.

It sounds plausible, but there's just one problem. The "copycat" is rarely able to achieve the same success. Let me qualify that statement. It is always beneficial when you incorporate the universal principles that successful people apply.

Universal principles, such as positive attitude, persistence, integrity, responsibility, and courage, work for everyone.

You'd be wise to "copy" these concepts. However, when you try to copy the specific *actions* or career path taken by someone else, you'll find that you won't get the same results the other person is getting. You may wonder how that could happen. If someone gives me the "recipe" for success, why can't I just follow what that person did — and get the same successful results?

Perhaps an example will help illustrate this point. Let's assume ABC Insurance Company has a highly successful salesperson (named "Phil") who is outselling other sales-people by a wide margin. We find out that Phil picks up the phone and makes cold calls to prospects using a script to schedule appointments. If we gave that "winning" script to another salesperson in the company (called "Joe"), there is no guarantee that Joe would get the same results. But how can that happen? After all, Joe is modeling what Phil did.

Success is more than just doing things. There are mental and emotional components to success. You can't tap into the precise mental and emotional capabilities of other people. They have a different confidence level. They have a different level of self-esteem. They have different talents and interests. They give off a distinct vibration, which is not the same as your vibration. The persons who interact with these individuals feel these "intangibles" and respond accordingly.

You achieve success from the inside-out. When you don't believe you will be successful and don't have the positive feelings that successful people have, you can't "copy" their success by imitating their words or actions. You will inevitably get results that are consistent with your own beliefs and emotions. Thus, if Joe doesn't believe he can be successful, or if he feels he doesn't deserve success, he will attain results that confirm his limiting beliefs. Joe might use the same words as Phil while on the phone, but the listener may sense that Joe doesn't believe in himself, or that Joe doesn't believe in the product he is selling. Accordingly, the prospect may schedule an appointment with Phil, but decline Joe's invitation for a meeting.

There's another reason why "copying" others is not a wise strategy for you to use. When you copy someone else, you are not making use of the unique talents you possess. You access your power and maximize your potential by developing your own talents and being true to your own personality. When you copy someone else, people know that you are not being authentic. They may not be able to put their finger on it, but something just won't seem right.

On the other hand, when you express your own talents and personality, people are more at ease with you. They are more apt to like you and to do business with you. Furthermore, you came to this earth with skills that are uniquely yours to express. Nobody else can develop these talents or express them in exactly the same way that you can. This is your advantage — the area where no one can "compete" with you. You'll also find that when you follow your unique path, you'll begin to attract opportunities that are "tailor made" for you! These opportunities are more valuable than anything you could attempt to "copy" from someone else.

I'm not suggesting that we completely ignore what successful people do. We can learn some things from their actions. In our insurance example, perhaps Joe could make some changes to Phil's script to suit his own style and personality. Thus, the concept of using a script could be effective, even for Joe. However, Joe needs to adapt that concept in a way that uses his own personality, his own values, and his own special talents.

By all means, you should take advantage of the insights and experiences of others. That is why mentoring is so valuable. Copy the positive attitude and belief system of successful people. Learn how they use their emotions and feelings to get extraordinary results. However, when it comes to taking action and making decisions to move you forward, be an original. Tune into your own guidance system. Use your background, unique perspective, and abilities to your advantage. Don't be a copycat. Have the courage to do it your way, and you will be richly rewarded.

56

Giving and Receiving

Getters don't get — givers get.

— Eugene Benge

From the time we're young, we hear that "it's better to give than to receive." The implication is that there's something noble about giving, while there's something selfish about receiving. Don't get me wrong. I place the utmost importance on giving. There's much truth to the Biblical phrase, "Give and it shall be given unto you." In fact, giving is a prerequisite to receiving.

But let's not shortchange the role of receiving, either. To maximize our success and experience life to the fullest, we must learn how to give AND receive. Here are nine powerful guidelines for enhancing the quality of your life through both giving and receiving:

1. **Expand your view about giving.** Some people think of giving solely in the context of money ... and, indeed, many individuals do donate funds to worthy causes or organizations. However, you can also give of your *time* by volunteering. You can share your *knowledge* by serving as a mentor to a co-worker or a youngster. And let's not overlook one of the most important

ways to give—simply by *listening* attentively to another person.

2. **Consider the spirit in which you give.** Do you give grudgingly ... and with the hope that you'll get a quick return on your "investment?" Or, do you give just for the satisfaction you get from giving and because of your willingness to serve others? When you give cheerfully and without expectation of return, you'll reap many tangible and intangible benefits over the long haul.

3. **There are no small acts of giving.** Don't overlook the seemingly small, everyday acts of giving. A smile to a cashier or a few words of encouragement to a co-worker—those are significant acts of giving. Simply put, giving is not limited to donating large sums of money where they name a wing of a hospital after you. So, resist the temptation to judge one type of giving as superior to another. Take advantage of *every* opportunity you have to make someone's day a little easier.

4. **Be a giver and not a taker.** Of course, every person thinks of himself or herself as a "giver" as opposed to a "taker." But the way others perceive us is often to the contrary. This isn't an "all or nothing" issue. Sometimes, we get out of balance and don't even realize we're crossing the line from giver to taker. Frequently, we do this when we're in need of help, such as finding a new job. What others can do for us suddenly becomes the focus of our conversations. Be brutally honest with yourself. In networking situations and with co-workers or clients, make absolutely certain that you're taking an active interest in *serving* others—as opposed to pushing your own agenda most of the time. By all means ask for help when you

need it. But recognize that people are less likely to help "takers," whereas they'll willingly help "givers."

5. **Give to yourself by saying "NO."** Our final tip for how to give may surprise you. You see, giving to *yourself* is also important. Sometimes, we think we have to help others whenever they ask for our assistance. Not so! When you do that, you stretch yourself too thin and get burned out. It's essential that you honor yourself by declining some requests that are made on your time and your resources.

   Now that we've looked at some fundamental principles of **giving**, let's turn our attention to the equally important skill of **receiving**.

6. **Receive all compliments willingly.** Some people can easily give compliments to others, but when it comes to being on the receiving end of praise, they're very uncomfortable and will often "reject" the compliment. *"You did a great job with that account"* is often followed by *"Oh, I really didn't do anything."* From this point on, no matter what compliment you receive, just say *"thank you."* If someone says you're the nicest person on earth, don't get into a debate about the merits of the comment. Just accept it with *"thank you."* When you reject compliments, you rob others of the satisfaction of giving to you and diminish your own value and self-esteem.

7. **Receive all material gifts willingly.** If someone offers you a gift *without any strings attached*, accept it. (NOTE: When this occurs within a business setting, be sure that your organization doesn't have a rule prohibiting the receipt of such gifts.) Here again, it's important to allow others to give to you. They do so because of the satisfaction they get from this act (and because they feel you deserve this gift). Allow them

to have that satisfaction ... and pay enough value to yourself to believe that you deserve it.

8. **Be grateful for what you've already received.** Simply put, gratitude enhances receiving. The more you appreciate what you've already received, the more you'll receive in the future. So, stop taking the many gifts in your life for granted. Your health, your loved ones, your material possessions. Appreciate these things on a daily basis and you'll receive even more!

9. **Receiving requires patience.** If you've been a generous, cheerful giver, you *will* receive. Unfortunately, I can't tell you when it will happen ... or where it will come from. The universe takes care of these details— and in ways that you could never predict. The people you give to are not necessarily the people who will give back to you. But rest assured that giving creates a boomerang, and in the long run, you'll receive in equal or greater measure to what you have given.

Years ago, I heard an audio program by Robert Schuller in which he said: "You really can't give anything away. It will always come back to you." Isn't that a magnificent concept? And I've found it to be true. Giving is wonderful on many accounts. The real joy in life comes from being of service to others. It gives us a feeling of satisfaction, knowing that our lives make a difference. However, just as we want to give to others, we must allow others to give to us.

So, become a cheerful giver and a willing receiver. It's a prescription for a happy, meaningful, and successful life.

57

When Are We Going to Get There?

There are no shortcuts to any place worth going.

— Beverly Sills

W hen I was a young boy, our family used to take car trips. Sometimes, we'd travel from New York to some of the southern states. Occasionally, we went to Canada. My father always did the driving, my mom sat in the front passenger seat, and my brother and I sat in the back. We'd be about 30 miles into our 500 mile journey when I'd start to squirm and ask my father, "When are we going to get there?"

My dad would say that we'd just gotten started and had plenty left to go. And 40 or 50 miles later, (maybe even less!) I'd ask the same question. Of course, we always got there eventually, and I survived each trip. I guess I was just a little impatient.

I got to thinking about some of my goals recently and once again, I heard myself asking, "When am I going to get there?" Do you ask yourself that same question when it comes to your goals? Maybe you've been working so hard to get a particular result ... and it just hasn't happened yet.

If you ever find yourself in that position, here's a little encouragement and some points to reflect upon. Please understand, however, that nobody else has the answers to your challenges. These are some issues to consider, but it is **you** who ultimately must make your own decisions.

1. **Re-assess your PQ (Passion Quotient).** Are you still excited about attaining this goal? If so, keep forging ahead. However, if you've lost your enthusiasm for the goal, maybe it's time to re-evaluate the road you're on. You can fool yourself with rational arguments about why you're doing what you're doing. But I've learned that *gut feelings* don't lie. If every day is a struggle and brings little satisfaction, you're going to drain yourself physically, emotionally and spiritually.

   Careful here. I'm **not** saying that every task along the way will be fun. That's rarely the case. But, if at the end of each day, you find yourself saying, "I really hate doing this," you should think long and hard about making some changes.

2. **Enjoy the sights along the way.** During my childhood car trips, I was so focused on the signs posting the number of miles to our destination that I neglected to see—and appreciate—the beautiful scenery along the way. And so it is with our lives. If we become too preoccupied with the end result, we miss many of the precious moments that make up our days, months and years. We don't appreciate our family and we don't see all of the beauty and miracles that surround us. So, don't let the pursuit of your goal cause you to lose your balance and to shut out everything else in your world.

3. **Give yourself credit for the distance you've already traveled.** We often focus all of our energy on the things we feel are missing ... the goals we *haven't*

yet attained. And we forget about the many things we *have* accomplished. If you have some ambitious goals, I'll bet that you've already had some extraordinary accomplishments along the way. Think of where you were five or ten years ago ... or even two years ago. Give yourself a pat on the back for the skills you developed, the commitment you've demonstrated, the lives you've affected and the results you've achieved.

4. **Have lots of patience.** Years ago, I heard an audio program by Wayne Dyer in which he said, "Great things have no fear of time." What a marvelous approach! If you believe in yourself at the deepest level, you're going to continue until you accomplish what you set out to do. Sometimes, it will take much longer than you thought. As David Geffen once said, "There's God's plan and your plan. And your plan doesn't matter." Take the example of actor William H. Macy, who earned an Oscar nomination in 1997 for his performance in the movie, *Fargo*. Macy's breakthrough came at the age of 47, after he had been acting for more than 25 years, mostly in plays. There were times he thought about giving up on his acting career. Now, he's in demand as one of the top actors in the business. So, hang in there and be patient.

5. **Realize that getting "there" won't make you happy.** It's easy to fall into this trap. You get so obsessed with achieving something in your business that you begin to get the crazy idea that reaching the goal will bring you instant happiness. Yet, the very moment of reaching your goal is seldom the euphoria you think it will be. Tennis star Martina Navratilova offered this insight: "The moment of victory is much too short to live for that and nothing else." You experience real joy and build character from the entire journey toward

your goal. Besides, let's not forget that when you **do** get "there," you still must choose another "there" to pursue.

6. **Make some progress every day.** It's so easy to get down and discouraged when things aren't going as we had planned. And it's okay to get down … for a few minutes. Then, pick yourself up and make sure, each day, to do *a few things* that will move you toward your objective. They don't have to be monumental tasks—even a phone call or a letter counts. This will keep your momentum rolling, and you'll discover the rewards that come from being disciplined and taking constructive actions day in and day out. The worst thing you can do is sit back, do nothing and feel sorry for yourself.

7. **Be flexible and ready to take a detour.** In the 1980s, self-help writers often advocated setting 10 or 20 year goals. My, how the world has changed! Now, we know how difficult it is to predict the business climate and technological advances that will occur within the next few *months*. With this rapid change, however, comes incredible new opportunities, and we must be prepared to seize them. That's why it's so important to be flexible about how you achieve your goals … and perhaps even about your goals themselves. You must have the courage to change highways when the timing seems right. Often the path you planned to take is not the same one you'll wind up on. Be open to new possibilities!

8. **Look for positive signs, however small.** We all have days where the phone doesn't ring and nothing seems to go right. If this is happening to you for weeks and months, it's probably time to re-assess your strategy. But if you're making progress, even slowly, life will

give you some signs, usually in the form of "minor" victories. You may close a significant sale ... meet an important contact ... or receive some gratifying feedback. Use these positive signs to inspire you to go even further!

I wish I could tell you how much longer it will be until *you* get to wherever it is you want to go. But I can't. From time to time, you're still going to get frustrated and ask this question. That's okay. Use these guidelines to keep you on track and help you to see things in the right perspective.

Remember, the journey is what really counts. Be sure to cherish every step along the way.

58

You're Making a
Lasting Impression

There's no such thing as a small act of kindness.
Every act creates a ripple with no logical end.

— Scott Adams

One of the earliest memories I have of my father is from one of the family vacations we took together. I was about 7 years old at the time, and we were driving somewhere in the southern United States. My brother and I were in the back of the car, with my mom and dad in the front. It was mid-afternoon on a hot summer day when my dad saw an ice cream truck and pulled over.

As my father got out of the car, he saw a group of five young boys sitting on the curb near the truck. Four of the five boys were eating ice cream. I watched as my dad went over to the boy without the ice cream and said to him, "Would you like some ice cream? I'll buy one for you." The boy politely told my father that he didn't want any.

Sure, it was a nice gesture on the part of my dad. But it wasn't a big deal, right?

Well ... actually, it was.

My father's act of kindness toward a complete stranger was imprinted on my mind that day. And I believe that my own conduct has been significantly shaped by that event.

My dad made a lasting impression on me in another way as well. You see, social or economic status meant very little to my father. He didn't gravitate to those with fancy titles. He seemed just as interested in speaking to waiters and the people who swept the floors. He respected everyone and looked down on nobody. And again, my dad's conduct helped to influence the way that I deal with people to this day.

Here are a few things to consider if you want to make a lasting impression and be a positive influence on others:

1. **Recognize the paradox.** We don't usually make a lasting impression when we're trying to do so. Rather, it happens when we're just living our lives and doing what may seem like ordinary, everyday things. Sure, there are some who make an enduring impact through great achievement or by being a celebrity. But lasting impressions are not reserved for famous people like Oprah Winfrey or Michael Jordan. They're available to you and me—every day, every moment.

   As I look back, I can't remember a time when my dad sat down with me and said, "Here's how you should treat people." I simply observed how he lived his life. So, too, people are watching your life, whether you realize it or not. This is true in all the life roles you play—be it parent, child, employee, business owner, etc.

2. **Live each moment consciously.** While we can't plan those encounters or situations that will create lasting impressions, we can be more aware of our behavior and the potential influence it may have. Too often, we live our lives on "automatic pilot," that is, we do things out of habit without realizing the effect our actions might have on others. In many of these instances, our behavior does not match what

we declare to be our values. (For instance, you may think that you are "open-minded" and then catch yourself being intolerant of someone with different viewpoints.)

Starting today, right now, realize that every interaction you have is precious. As author Dan Millman often says, "there are no ordinary moments." With this in mind, you can consciously choose, for example, to be honest, kind and to give your best efforts at all times.

So, the next time you're about to do something, ask yourself: What action would I take right now if I knew my behavior would have a lasting effect on someone? This isn't about being perfect. There will always be times when we behave in ways that we're not proud of. Yet, as you realize the impact of your day-to-day conduct, you'll find yourself making different choices.

3. **Appreciate the ripple effect.** It's hard to fathom the consequences of the lasting impressions we make. When my father asked that young boy whether he wanted some ice cream, he was affecting me—as well as everyone who would eventually come into contact with me—forever! Isn't that incredible? Yet, it's not an exaggeration. My dad's act helped to shape my character, which in turn affects the way that I have dealt with people in the 45 years since that event. Furthermore, the people who I have met may have been affected and have passed along those values to others they have met. It's an endless cycle. Thus, there are no small acts in this world. One simple act can truly change the course of humanity.

In the end, you're going to make many lasting impressions, whether you want to or not. It's up to you whether the messages you send are positive or negative. As you go through your day today, give a little extra consideration to how you speak and how you act. You just may be making an impression that will endure for generations.

59

The Path of Growth

It's what you learn after you know it all that counts.
— John Wooden

I f you're reading this article, I think it's safe to assume you're interested in self-development. I'm guessing you're not exactly the same person you were five years ago. You think differently. You act differently. You see the world differently. In short, you're growing and evolving.

When we're growing physically, we can see the changes. But when it comes to personal and professional growth, it's not always as easy to gauge our progress. Obviously, there's no simple test we can take to assess personal growth. But I've come up with some signposts that we can use to gain insight into where we stand.

See how many of the following items are true for you now. If they are, congratulations! And, if they're not, try implementing these concepts as you strive to reach the next level in your self-development.

1. **You don't fix blame or make excuses.** You realize more and more that pointing the finger at others is not the answer to your problems. Instead, you take personal responsibility for your own results and your own happiness. You focus on *your* attitude, *your* skills, *your* actions and *your* discipline.

2. **You don't look back.** Dwelling on unpleasant events in the past won't change them — and it only makes you feel rotten in the present. So why do it? Part of accepting personal responsibility is the recognition that, at any point, you can change the path you're on. Learn from the past, but don't obsess on it. Instead, take action today to create a positive future.

3. **You guard the sanctity of your thoughts.** You no longer doubt that your thoughts are creating your reality. And, if that's the case, why would you ever think negatively? You're disciplining yourself to focus on what you want — as opposed to what you don't want.

4. **Your spiritual beliefs are growing by leaps and bounds.** Once you've accepted the fact that a Higher Power created you and has a specific plan for your life, you begin to live life at a different level. You tune into your possibilities and have faith that you'll receive guidance during your journey. You take bold action. And, you're finding that you have the strength to handle the setbacks and disappointments that temporarily block your path.

5. **You stop comparing yourself with others.** You no longer judge your own success by how much money someone else is making or how fast you climbed the ladder in your organization. You compete only with yourself and aim to develop your own talents every day.

6. **You have a sense of gratitude every day.** When you're young, you tend to take everything for granted — your health, the roof over your head, and the food on your plate. As the years go by, you suddenly experience the "darker" side of life. Either you, or your relatives or friends face serious illnesses. You personally know people in their 30s, 40s or 50s who die. Instead of

complaining about the things in your life that aren't perfect, you choose to be thankful for the many gifts you've been given. You identify with the sage advice of Eddie Rickenbacker, who once said, "if you have all the fresh water you want to drink and all the food you want to eat, you should never complain about anything."

7. **You laugh a lot more — especially at yourself.** Several times each day, you find yourself letting out a hearty belly laugh. You take your work seriously but not yourself. Whether you're with clients, colleagues, friends or family, make sure to laugh. You'll feel better and have a lot more fun.

8. **You're excited about something.** When you're living in the flow of life and up to your highest potential, you're enthused. You don't have to go around slapping people on the back, but you're upbeat and alive. You get up in the morning with a purpose and you look forward to the day's activities. People can just look at you — or speak with you — and immediately pick up on your positive energy.

9. **You're taking some risks.** No one is asking you to go skydiving or put your physical health at risk. However, the path of growth demands that you venture into the unknown. That's where you discover yourself — and find out what you're capable of achieving. You begin to get ideas and visions about great things you can accomplish, and you have the courage to go after them. Instead of just thinking about doing something, you take action and do it!

10. **You're less concerned with what other people think.** Do you still need to get someone's approval before making a decision? On the path of growth, you're willing to do what *you* think is best for you — even

if someone else won't like it. On fundamental issues such as your career, your relationships and your goals, it's fine to get advice. But in the end, it's *your* view that counts. You'll never be happy following someone else's plan for your life.

11. **You place more emphasis on honesty and integrity.** Even when no one is looking, you do the right thing. Your aim is to build solid long-term relationships, both personally and professionally, and you can't accomplish this unless you're a person of character and integrity. Aside from being good to others, this is for your own self-interest. You see, whatever you send out in life will come back to you like a boomerang. So, if you want people to treat you with honesty and respect, you must treat them the same way.

12. **You stop trying to "fix" others.** You've learned that a little self-development can be dangerous. While you've begun to see that there's a better way to live and you're anxious for others to "see the light" as well, you recognize that everyone has their own path to follow — and that *you* don't decide the rate at which someone else progresses. So, instead of "converting" others, you continue to work on yourself and find that your example is more powerful than any sermon you can preach.

13. **You take the opportunity to lift someone else.** You remember how tough it was for you at each level of your life and your career, and how challenging it is right now. Furthermore, you know that you are where you now are, in large part, because some people believed in you ... encouraged you ... and helped you. You make a point to do the same for those who can benefit from your experience.

14. **You see things in perspective.** Your list of what's truly important in your life continues to shrink. You work hard and enjoy whatever material comforts you have, but "things" are not as essential to you as they once were. You recognize that the health and well-being of you and your loved ones is what really matters. You no longer let little day-to-day annoyances (at work or at home) ruin your entire day.

15. **You listen more ... and ask questions.** You've learned to tame your ego a bit and don't feel the need to always be the center of attention. You also realize that when you're talking, you're not learning anything. So, you balance your conversations and make sure to draw other people out by asking questions. You're more interested in learning about *their* backgrounds, *their* thoughts on various issues, *their* careers and *their* families. Every person has a fascinating story to tell, and you want to hear it.

16. **You've found that discipline is fun.** I never thought I'd say that! Yet it's true. To build physical fitness, you exercise several times each week. To develop a successful sales career, you pay attention to the basics, day in and day out. You're no longer looking for the "quick fix." Instead, you know full well that you must put in the effort before you can reap the reward. You find tremendous satisfaction in sticking with something and mastering it over a period of time.

17. **You set high standards for yourself and others.** Careful, this isn't about achieving "perfection." Rather, on the path of growth, you simply have the desire to reach more and more of your potential. You no longer settle for less than your best effort. And, as you see more of the potential in others, you encourage them to develop their talents as well.

We've now covered 17 signposts on your road to personal and professional growth. I'm sure you can add several more items as well, based on your own experiences. Keep these ideas in front of you on a regular basis to check on your progress. Apply them consistently and you'll enjoy phenomenal results — plus a tremendously exciting journey!

60

The Answers You Seek
Lie Within

Nobody has your answers.
— Jeff Keller

L ife would be much simpler if, when faced with a decision, we could easily consult with the ideal person or reference book and find the perfect solution. Unfortunately, it's seldom that easy.

There are no books, courses or sages that can make fundamental life decisions *for* you, choices such as: *Should I accept a new position in my company and relocate? ...* or *Should I marry this person?* Ultimately, these vital decisions are in your hands.

While your answers will ultimately be found within you, they may be difficult to access. What follows, then, is a set of guidelines to help you arrive at — and implement — successful solutions to the crucial issues in your life.

1. **Have faith in your abilities.** At any given moment, the choices you see as possible are directly related to what you *believe* you can achieve. If you lack a strong belief in your own abilities and envision yourself achieving merely limited success, your mind can

only access those answers which correspond to this limited vision. So, elevate your concept of what's possible for you — you'll become aware of far greater opportunities.

2. **Be decisive.** Most decisions, even important ones, are *not* life and death matters. Yet, many people get stuck because they try to figure out every variable before making up their minds. It's far better to choose one course and move forward. If your decision doesn't work out, you can make an adjustment or select a different option in the future. *(Note: I wouldn't use this approach in choosing a spouse!)*

    I'm not advocating taking hasty actions without research and planning. But, you can't wait for the "perfect" answer to show itself, with all of the difficulties and challenges worked out beforehand.

3. **Make sure you're considering what's best for *you*.** If you base your decisions on what others want you to do, you're headed for a life of frustration. You will never be fulfilled reaching someone else's goal. No one else can know the strengths and talents that lie within you. (In many cases, *you're* not even aware of them!) So, follow your heart's desires. That's where your power lies — and where you'll find your most fulfilling solutions.

4. **Recognize that answers are often revealed step-by-step.** In many ways, your life is like a jigsaw puzzle, with one piece inserted at a time. It is only after you start connecting some pieces that you can see how the others will fit into "the big picture." Frequently, you will receive an answer that will take you only to a certain point. Be content with that. As you implement that portion of the puzzle, you will grow and see the next appropriate action to take.

5. **Listen to your intuition.** Have you ever had a gut feeling that something wasn't right — and went ahead with it anyway? How did it turn out? Chances are, you later regretted your decision. Your intuition tried to warn you that something was wrong, and you ignored it. Trust your intuition and follow its guidance — even if the apparent answer goes against your preconceived notions.

6. **Pray and seek spiritual guidance.** Many people find that they can access the "right" answers from their connection to a Higher Power. This isn't about pleading for a specific result. Instead, maintain an open mind and ask your Higher Power to guide you in making key decisions.

7. **Be willing to implement the answer.** Many people know the answer to their problem but are simply not willing to do what it takes to go forward with the solution. For instance, you might have a long-standing employee who is performing poorly. You know that you should fire that person, but you just can't bring yourself to do it.

   Recognize that your best answers will often involve challenges, obstacles and, possibly, some emotional distress. That's the price you'll have to pay, but in the long run, you'll be glad you did.

8. **Be courageous!** Courage is the one trait that will almost guarantee that you access your most powerful answers and implement them successfully. Have the courage to explore the limits of your potential and to act on the answers that emerge. Be willing to fail along the way. As you demonstrate your courage, life will reward you with more and more fantastic answers and opportunities.

Your life is a journey to discover and develop your unique strengths. Go forward with courage, high expectations, persistence, and a willingness to be true to yourself. Then, you'll find all the answers you need.

61

Everything Happens
for a Reason

*All that I have seen teaches me
to trust the Creator for all I have not seen.*

— Ralph Waldo Emerson

Would you like to enjoy more success and have less stress in your life? Do you wish that your daily aggravations had less power over you? Would you appreciate some peace of mind?

No, you don't need to find a genie in a bottle to enjoy these spectacular benefits. What you do need, however, is a belief in one key concept — that *everything happens for a reason.*

When I began speaking before groups more than 20 years ago, I often asked the members of my audience, "How many of you believe that everything happens for a reason?" Typically, about 25% of the people would raise their hands. Now, when I ask that same question, anywhere from 50% to 80% of the audience answers in the affirmative.

Whether you already believe that things happen for a purpose, or are unsure about this notion, here are some points to consider to get the maximum results from this principle:

1. **Don't curse your present circumstances ... or gripe about the past.** When we encounter "negative" or stressful situations in our lives, our immediate reaction is to be outraged, frustrated or depressed. This is the start of a downward spiral in which we fill our minds with gloomy thoughts and generate more negative results. On the contrary, when you believe there's a purpose for your difficulties, your state of mind is quite different. You realize that your current situation is serving you in some way, whether it's a turn in the road or a lesson that you can apply at a later date.

2. **This principle is not limited to tragedies and problems.** While it's true that you can find positive aspects to every setback, the idea that everything happens for a reason applies to positive experiences and "neutral" events as well. For instance, let's say that you meet someone at a networking meeting. The person holds no special significance to you and doesn't seem likely to bring you any business. What you're not considering are the possible ways that the two of you might help each other in the future.

3. **Being passive is not the answer.** Just because there is a "reason" for the events that happen to you doesn't mean you can achieve your goals by sitting back and waiting for success to occur on its own. It's still up to you to be proactive and make things happen. That requires energy, creativity and, yes, a lot of effort on your part!

4. **Recognize the "two way street."** It's easy to get caught up with the idea that every person you meet has something to contribute to you. That's true *to some extent*. But, don't overlook the fact that there is something for you to impart to others as well.

And, while there are often ways in which each party contributes to the other, there are many instances where it's not an equal "give and take." Thus, there are times in a relationship when you may be *serving* another person more often than you are *receiving* from them.

5. **You are always being directed toward something "better."** Have you ever been fired from a job ... then moved on to find a better career? Or, have you terminated a personal relationship (or been terminated yourself!) ... and then met someone who was a far better partner for you? In both of these instances, life was pushing you toward something that would bring you even more satisfaction.

    Of course, in all of these situations, you had the option to close off the improved alternative. For instance, after being fired, you could have complained about the lack of job opportunities. Or, after the relationship ended, you could have concluded that you are "unlucky in love." Yet, had you taken these approaches, you would have missed the better situation that was just around the corner.

6. **You'll never be able to explain *everything*.** The notion that everything happens for a reason will not answer every question that you have about life. On the contrary, although you'll find that you are better able to understand certain events, there will still be many mysteries that you can't explain.

There are no coincidences. When you believe this, you'll enter a new world of possibility. When a problem occurs, instead of crying, "Why Me?" you'll look for the lesson you can learn, or the opportunity that is on the horizon.

You'll realize that it makes no sense to argue that something shouldn't have happened to you. It did happen ... there's a reason for it ... and, if you're wise, you'll use it to your advantage!

62

Let's Start
Some New Trends

It seems we're always in transition and that it's more
about trends than it is about what's meaningful.

— Marlee Matlin

When someone talks about "trends," you might think of the stock market or the kinds of dresses or ties that are in style now. But I believe there are more important, and less discussed, trends at work in our everyday lives. The trends I'm referring to are the principles we live by. And some of these trends are very disturbing indeed.

Here are some new trends I'd like to substitute for those that seem to be in vogue now:

Taking Responsibility ... instead of ... Blame and Excuses. We're living at a time when finger pointing has become all too common and personal responsibility is on the wane. If we make poor choices, we should accept the consequences of those choices. If we're looking to find scapegoats, we'll never be successful or happy. We are in charge of the direction of our lives. When we take responsibility, we can make positive changes. When we blame others, we stay stuck.

Honoring Every Individual ... instead of ... Celebrity Worship. It's bad enough that we spend countless hours watching mindless shows on TV. But what's the point of following the personal lives of movie or TV stars? Why read about their lives — or watch gossip shows on TV — while we could be concentrating instead of developing our own talents or doing something else worthwhile? Personally, I don't believe anyone is "better" or "more important" than anyone else. We're all on an equal plane, regardless of your job or the size of your bank account. Is the dedicated school teacher who is molding your child's life any less important that the star of a TV sitcom? I think it's time to stop obsessing about celebrities and start valuing every person who crosses our paths.

Authenticity ... instead of ... Saying What You Think Others Want to Hear. It's a challenge to find people who say what they really believe. Take politicians for example. They are rarely authentic and will only say what is "politically correct," often guided by the last poll taken. You also see this lack of authenticity and reality in the way businesses portray themselves. Consider the insurance company commercials you watch on TV. We see a scenario where the agent arrives at the scene of the accident immediately to help the client pull his car out of the water and also arranges for payment to be made on the claim the same week. Do you believe this is the way most claims are handled?

While it's true that we all (individuals and businesses) wear a "mask" to some degree and often portray ourselves as something we are not, we can benefit by being more authentic. This, in turn, would allow us to communicate more effectively with others and also feel better about ourselves. Authenticity is a powerful force if we have the courage to embrace it.

Tolerance of Ideas ... instead of ... Confrontation and Rigidity. I was always taught that you could disagree with someone without being disagreeable. That philosophy seems to have gone out the window. It has been replaced by a combative stance where people aggressively attack others who disagree with their positions. On the TV news programs, you often see guests who are advocating different sides of an issue. The "debate" often turns to personal attacks and putting down the other person's views as ridiculous. A lot of talk radio is built on this premise. Yet, most issues in life are simply not "black" and "white" — and we can't expect others with different backgrounds and experiences to agree with our take on every issue. We need to listen more and be open to those who have different viewpoints. We just might learn that we don't know it all, and that the truth is often found in between extreme positions.

Positive Focus ... instead of ... Negative Focus. How much of what you read, see or hear in the media is positive? Maybe 10%. It's not the media's fault. The moment people stop watching or reading negative news, the media will offer something different. We've allowed ourselves to get in the habit of concentrating on the negative. Regardless of what the media reports, you can become a broadcaster of positive news. You can live your life talking about the positive rather than the negative. You can express gratitude for what you have instead of complaining about what you don't have. You can see the good in others rather than harping on their faults. When you shift your focus to the positive, you'll achieve more, feel better and inspire others.

Simplicity and spontaneity ... instead of ... excessive planning and structure. Life seemed a lot less complicated when I was a kid. After school, I did my homework and went outside or to the school yard to play sports with friends. Nowadays, it seems that every youngster has a multitude of scheduled activities to attend each day. These kids need day planners because their busy schedules rival that of a corporate executive. In addition, parents are expected to chauffeur the kids to and from these events. As a result, both the youngsters and the parents are stressed.

Yes, folks, I realize that the world is different today and that economic and social realities — two-working-parent families, day care centers, less safe neighborhoods, etc. — have altered the way our children are raised. And, in fact, many would argue that kids today have wider opportunities because they are exposed to all these activities. That said, call me "old fashioned" but I think there's inherent value in a life that doesn't have all that structure and allows for some spontaneity. Taking on more and more activities doesn't mean you lead a better life. It may be just the opposite.

Inner Peace ... instead of ... seeking outside stimulation. There's nothing wrong with excitement and external stimulation. However, when we think that things outside of ourselves are going to bring us lasting satisfaction, we're kidding ourselves. Peace and happiness can only be found within. No other person can bring you inner peace. No stimulant or drug will bring you peace. I'm all for material success; it makes your journey more enjoyable and allows you to help others. Yet, no amount of material wealth will bring you lasting contentment. Peace is developed through moments of quietness — not in the midst of pulsating noise and chaos — and not by stockpiling possessions.

Now that you've reviewed some of these trends, give some thought as to which ones will serve you. It is up to you to make a decision whether you want to participate in the current trends — or blaze a new trail. Let's take a final look at the new trends I'm suggesting:

- Taking Responsibility
- Honoring Every Individual
- Authenticity

◆Tolerance of Ideas

◆Positive Focus

◆Simplicity and Spontaneity

◆Inner Peace

When you follow these new trends, you'll create a life filled with meaning, connection and uncommon success.